WELCOME
TO THE
KINGDOM

AWAKEN TO YOUR DIVINE CITIZENSHIP

CHARLES E. MEUX, JR.

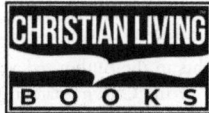

CHRISTIAN LIVING
B O O K S

Largo, MD

Christian Living Books, Inc.
christianlivingbooks.com
We bring your dreams to fruition.

ISBN 9781562295882

ENDORSEMENTS

Embrace the Kingdom of God with *Welcome to the Kingdom,* a life-changing book that will strengthen your faith and deepen your understanding of Jesus Christ's sacrifice. This essential guidebook is a must-read for believers at any stage of their journey, offering practical insights and spiritual guidance to help you tap into the transformative power of salvation. I extend a passionate invitation to all pastors and leaders to employ this as a teaching tool to inspire those who are embarking on their spiritual journey. We never tire of learning, and it is refreshing to reexamine the Word of God. Pastor Meux is committed to spreading the message of the Kingdom of God, and this book is a vital resource for all who seek to be part of this glorious mandate. With divine inspiration, he crafts each sentence with passion and purpose, shedding light on the path to positive change. Continued blessings and favor upon your work that it might make a great impact in the earth realm.

—Vicki L Kemp, Best Selling Author

I wholeheartedly endorse this remarkable book, *Welcome to the Kingdom,* which serves as a profound introduction to the Kingdom of God. With clarity and passion, Pastor Meux expertly explains the fundamental principles that define our faith, offering invaluable training that equips readers to fully embrace their role within God's Kingdom. This book is not only informative but also motivational, inspiring us to live out our faith with purpose and dedication. One cannot read this book and not be motivated to find their place, and purpose in God's divine plan for their life. I highly recommend it to anyone seeking to deepen their understanding and commitment to being part of the Kingdom of God.

—Bishop Darrell Dorris
Founder of Living Faith Cathedral
Presiding Bishop of Antelope Valley District of Churches

One of the greatest needs of the modern church has become the need for Bible-based discipleship. We have lacked in our ability to train the new while strengthening the old. *Welcome to the Kingdom* is a key that will assist new believers—as well as seasoned believers—in walking through the biblical process of regeneration and development in Christ. The Holy Spirit has led Pastor Charles Meux to write these practical and profound Kingdom truths that will further your walk with the Lord no matter what level of glory you find yourself in. Prepare to be edified and encouraged as you take this journey and are Welcomed into the Kingdom of our God.

—Apostle Nathaniel E. Leon
Senior Pastor of This Rock International Ministries
Overseer of Raising the Altar in the Nations

Pastor Charles Meux is a powerful Pastor, Prophet, and Teacher. God has given him the heartbeat of the Holy Spirit and an ear to hear the voice of God. This book is a powerful read and skillfully articulates Kingdom principles. It has the potential to transform a generation.

—Bishop Dr. Princeton L. Allen, Th.D., D.D
President of Ephraim Life Bible College and Seminary
Ventura, CA

DEDICATION

This book is dedicated to all the readers who are looking for spiritual and Godly inspiration, knowledge, and growth. Your endless pursuit of learning and self-improvement in biblical understanding motivates us to create material that will help you on your journey. As you read this book, I invite you to open your heart and mind to receive the messages within. May it be a source of inspiration, wisdom, and guidance as you continue your journey towards spiritual growth.

May this book bring you closer to God and inspire you to live a life full of purpose, love, and faith. May it serve as a reminder that no matter what challenges you face, God is always with you, guiding and strengthening you.

I dedicate this book to my lovely wife, Prophetess Desiree L. Meux, who has always been supportive of all my endeavors, to include this book. Without her love and encouragement, this project would not have been possible.

Lastly, but most importantly, this book is dedicated to God, the source of all inspiration, wisdom, and love. Without His grace and guidance, none of this would be possible. May this book bring glory to His name and spread His message of hope and salvation to all who read it. I pray that this book will touch your heart and soul as much as it has touched ours during its creation. May it be a source of encouragement and strength for you on your spiritual journey.

TABLE OF CONTENTS

INTRODUCTION

I am delighted that you have chosen to embark on this journey of personal growth and spiritual exploration. Whether you are new to faith or have been walking with God for many years, this book promises to bring you deeper understanding and joy in your relationship with Jesus Christ.

I've been walking with God for 15 years, and it has been the most rewarding journey of my life. While it hasn't always been easy, it has been filled with purpose, peace, and fulfillment beyond anything I could have imagined. When I gave my life to Christ, it was the best decision I had ever made. Let me add that choosing to follow Christ doesn't mean your life will become easier - you will still face life's challenges. However, you'll face them with hope in Jesus, and that hope becomes your comfort through every situation. Our foundation is firmly rooted in Scripture

> Nor is there salvation in any other, for there is no other name under heaven given among men by which we must be saved. (Acts 4:12)

This fundamental truth—that salvation comes through Jesus Christ alone—forms the cornerstone of our faith journey.

This truth is further illuminated in Romans:

> That if you shalt confess with your mouth the Lord Jesus, and shalt believe in thine heart that God hath raised him from the dead, thou shalt be saved. For with the heart man believeth unto righteousness, and with the mouth confession is made unto salvation. (Romans 10:9-10)

Through this confession of faith and belief in Christ's resurrection, we enter into a transformative relationship with God.

This book is designed to guide you through several essential aspects of faith. Each chapter builds upon the previous one, creating a comprehensive pathway for spiritual development. You'll find real-life examples, Scripture references, and practical applications to help you implement these truths in your daily life. I encourage you to take your time with this material. Read thoughtfully, reflect deeply, and most importantly, put into practice what you learn.

Keep a journal nearby to write down your thoughts, questions, and revelations as you read. These notes will become valuable touchstones in your spiritual journey. At the end of each chapter, you'll find prayer points— use these as starting points for your own conversations with God. Remember, prayer is simply talking with your Heavenly Father, who loves you and desires a relationship with you.

The companion *Welcome to the Kingdom Workbook* is available to further enhance your learning journey. It provides in-depth exercises, reflection questions, and practical applications for each chapter. This workbook will help you internalize these Kingdom principles and apply them to your daily life.

Following this introduction, you'll find a self-reflection guide. I encourage you to take time to complete it honestly. It will help you identify areas for growth and provide a baseline against which to measure your progress as you read the book.

Whether you're reading this book on your own, as part of a small group, or in preparation for ministry, my prayer is that it will spark a deeper passion for God in your heart. May it lead to meaningful conversations, deeper understanding, and most importantly, a closer walk with our Lord and Savior.

Let this book be more than just information—let it be a catalyst for transformation in your life. As you read, remain open to what the Holy Spirit wants to do in and through you. Every truth we explore together can become a living reality in your daily walk with God.

This is your journey. Don't rush through the process. Every step forward, no matter how small it may seem, is progress in your spiritual growth. Thank you for allowing me to be part of your journey through these pages. May God's grace guide you as you begin this adventure of discovering more of Him.

Now, let's take some time for personal reflection with the following guide. This isn't a test—it's a tool to help you get the most out of your journey through this book.

KINGDOM SELF-REFLECTION GUIDE

Now that you understand the importance of Kingdom citizenship, let's take time to reflect on your personal spiritual journey. This guide will help you explore where you are in your walk with Christ and how you might grow deeper in your Kingdom experience.

Beginning Your Kingdom Journey
- What drew you to learn more about God's Kingdom?
- What aspects of Kingdom citizenship most interest or challenge you?
- What questions do you have about living as a Kingdom citizen?

Your Relationship with Christ
- How would you describe your current relationship with Jesus Christ?
- If you are born again, when did you accept Christ? What led to that decision?
- What aspects of your faith feel strongest right now? Where do you feel you need growth?

Your Spiritual Foundation

- How familiar are you with the concept of salvation? What does it mean to you?
- Have you been baptized in water? If not, what questions do you have about baptism?
- How would you describe your understanding of the Holy Spirit's role in your life?
- Are you connected to a church community? If so, how has it impacted your faith journey?

Your Spiritual Practices

- Describe your current prayer life. How often do you pray and what does that look like?
- What is your approach to reading and studying the Bible? Do you have a regular routine?
- How do you practice giving/tithing? What are your beliefs about financial stewardship?
- How do you handle forgiveness? Are there areas where you struggle to forgive?

Your Character Development

- What aspects of your character do you feel align well with Christ's teachings?
- What areas of your character would you like to develop further?
- How do you handle life's challenges? Where do you turn for strength?

Your Kingdom Purpose

- What spiritual gifts or talents has God given you?
- How are you currently using these gifts to serve others?
- What areas of ministry or service interest you?

Looking Ahead

- After reading the Introduction, what topics are you most excited to learn about?
- What specific areas of your spiritual life would you like to focus on developing?
- What practical steps can you take to grow in these areas?
- Who can support and guide you in your spiritual journey?

Remember: This is not a test but a tool for personal reflection and growth. Be honest with yourself and with God. Use these questions as starting points for prayer and meditation, asking the Holy Spirit to guide your development as a citizen of God's Kingdom.

Consider keeping a journal of your responses and revisiting these questions periodically as you progress through this book and your Kingdom journey.

WELCOME TO THE KINGDOM WORKBOOK

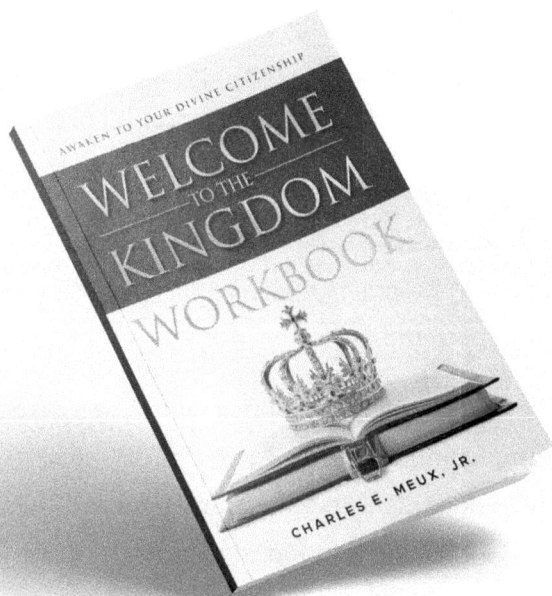

Transform Your Understanding into Powerful Application

Are you ready to move beyond surface-level Christianity to experience the full reality of God's Kingdom in your daily life? Based on Pastor Meux's transformative book "Welcome to the Kingdom," this comprehensive workbook provides the practical tools you need to apply Kingdom principles and see tangible results. Inside this interactive guide:

- Soul-searching questions that challenge you to examine your current spiritual position
- Practical exercises designed to activate Kingdom principles in real-life situations

- Scripture Memorization & Meditation practices to renew your mind
- Kingdom Territory Expansion strategies for claiming every area of your life for God's purposes
- Royal Declarations that align your words with Heaven's authority

Each chapter builds upon the main book's teachings, helping you establish God's rule and reign in your relationships, finances, character, prayer life, and every other dimension of your existence. It's perfect for…

- Individual spiritual growth journeys
- Small group Bible studies
- Church discipleship programs
- Ministry leadership training

Whether you're a new believer or a seasoned saint, this workbook will help you move from simply understanding Kingdom concepts to experiencing their transformative power. Begin your journey toward living as an empowered citizen of God's Kingdom today!

ISBN 9781562296506 | 8.5" x 11" | 60 pages | Paperback

Available wherever books are sold or from ChristianLivingBooks.com

CHAPTER ONE

WHAT IS THE KINGDOM OF GOD?

Welcome to the Kingdom of God! I invite you to consider this truth: understanding God's Kingdom is not optional for the believer who desires to walk in the fullness of Christ. It is the foundation upon which all transformation rests, the lens through which we perceive His plans, and the power by which Heaven's reality invades Earth. The Kingdom is not a distant hope but a present reality that beckons us to align with its principles and live as citizens of Heaven here and now.

The Greek word for "Kingdom" is basileia, which means royal power, dominion, rule, and authority. It is not just a place; it is the dynamic reign of God, bringing order where there was chaos, healing where there was brokenness, and life where there was death. When Jesus said, "Seek first the Kingdom of God and His righteousness" (Matthew 6:33), He was not giving a religious suggestion but revealing the key to unlocking Heaven's abundance on Earth. He was inviting us into a life where God's

rule is supreme, and His purposes become our highest pursuit.

Scripture tells us that after His resurrection, Jesus spent forty days speaking to His disciples about "the things pertaining to the Kingdom of God" (Acts 1:3). Why did He devote such focused attention to this subject? Because the Kingdom was central to His mission. It was not merely a theological concept but the reality He demonstrated through miracles, teaching, and the laying down of His life.

When Jesus healed the sick, cast out demons, and raised the dead, He revealed what happens when God's Kingdom collides with Earth. He showed us the culture of Heaven—a place where sickness has no power, darkness has no claim, and death has no sting. Then, He commissioned us to do the same: "As the Father has sent Me, I also send you" (John 20:21).

> **HE REVEALED WHAT HAPPENS WHEN GOD'S KINGDOM COLLIDES WITH EARTH.**

This is the essence of Kingdom living: to carry the realities of Heaven into the broken places of Earth. It is not about escaping to Heaven someday; it is about partnering with God to bring His rule and reign into every sphere of life today.

The Culture of the Kingdom

The culture of God's Kingdom operates on fundamentally different principles than earthly systems. At its very foundation is divine love—the Greek word agape. This is not a fleeting emotion but the supernatural love that flows from God Himself. It is the love that transforms how we:

- ♛ Relate to God (intimacy rather than religious duty)
- ♛ View others (as valuable image-bearers rather than tools or obstacles)
- ♛ Handle conflicts (seeking reconciliation rather than revenge)

- ♛ Make decisions (choosing what benefits others rather than just ourselves)
- ♛ Use resources (stewarding them for Kingdom purposes rather than selfish gain)

When we embrace this culture, our lives become living testimonies of the King we serve. People will see the difference, not because we are striving to appear holy, but because the reality of God's Kingdom is shaping every part of who we are.

Truth and Kingdom Integrity

Truth and integrity are non-negotiable in the Kingdom. Proverbs 11:3 declares, "The integrity of the upright will guide them, but the perversity of the unfaithful will destroy them." The Hebrew word for integrity, tom, speaks of completeness, fullness, and moral innocence. Kingdom integrity means:

- ♛ Aligning with God's Word regardless of circumstances
- ♛ Living transparently before God and others
- ♛ Keeping commitments even when it costs us
- ♛ Speaking truth in love
- ♛ Refusing to live with pretense or hypocrisy

This level of integrity is not possible in human strength. It flows from abiding in Christ, allowing His truth to saturate our hearts and transform our character.

Righteousness and Justice

In the Kingdom, righteousness and justice are inseparable. The Greek word for righteousness is dikaiosyne, which means right standing with

God, right living, and right relationships. It is not merely about personal morality but about embodying the values of Heaven.

Romans 2:11 reminds us, "For there is no partiality with God." This truth calls us to:

- Advocate for the oppressed
- Treat all people with honor and dignity
- Live empowered by the Spirit to do what is right
- Stand for justice even when it is costly

The Kingdom is a place where every voice matters, and every life carries immeasurable value. As ambassadors of this Kingdom, we are called to reflect God's heart for justice in a world that desperately needs it.

Humility and Honor

"Let nothing be done through selfish ambition or conceit, but in lowliness of mind let each esteem others better than himself" (Philippians 2:3). Humility is the foundation of Kingdom greatness. It is the posture that allows us to receive grace and walk in God's power. In the Kingdom, honor flows naturally from humility. What does that look like?

- Recognizing and respecting authority
- Preferring others above ourselves
- Serving without seeking recognition
- Receiving correction with grace
- Giving credit to others while taking responsibility for our actions

When we walk in humility and honor, we create an atmosphere where God's presence can dwell and His purposes can flourish.

Faith and Obedience

Faith in the Kingdom is not passive; it is active trust expressed through obedience. Proverbs 3:5 exhorts us to "Trust in the Lord with all your heart, and lean not on your own understanding." This kind of faith involves:

- Absolute confidence in God's character
- Unwavering reliance on His promises
- Immediate response to His direction
- Courage to step out even when the path is unclear
- Perseverance in the face of opposition

Faith opens the door to the impossible. It allows us to partner with God in ways that defy human reasoning and bring Heaven's reality into the natural realm.

Kingdom Citizenship

When we receive salvation through Jesus Christ, we are not merely saved from something; we are saved into something. We become citizens of God's Kingdom. The Greek word for citizenship is politeuma, which speaks of the rights and responsibilities of belonging to a heavenly commonwealth. As Kingdom citizens, we are granted:

- Direct access to God's presence
- Authority in Christ's name
- Divine protection and provision
- Status as sons and daughters
- Access to Kingdom resources and power

This citizenship is not just a title; it is a transformational reality. It defines our identity and empowers us to live as ambassadors of Christ, representing His rule and reign in every sphere of influence.

Kingdom Practices in Daily Life

Kingdom living must be demonstrated through daily practices that reflect Heaven's culture. Worship is foundational to these practices. The Greek word for worship is proskuneo, which means to bow down in reverence and adoration. Worship is not confined to Sunday services; it is a lifestyle of continuous awareness of God's presence.

WE BECOME CITIZENS OF GOD'S KINGDOM.

Prayer and intercession deepen our connection to the King and expand our Kingdom impact. As we commune with God, we develop what Scripture calls parresia—holy boldness. This boldness empowers us to make declarations that align Earth with Heaven's purposes.

The Word of God is the cornerstone of Kingdom living. Matthew 4:4 declares, "Man shall not live by bread alone, but by every word that proceeds from the mouth of God." To live by the Word means to:

- Embrace it as our final authority
- Engage in regular study and meditation
- Apply its principles to our decisions
- Teach its truths to others
- Speak words that release life and hope

The Kingdom of God is not just a future promise; it is a present reality. Jesus told Nicodemus, "Unless one is born again, he cannot see the Kingdom of God" (John 3:3). To be born again is to be spiritually reborn, to experience a transformation that makes us citizens of Heaven while living on Earth.

As we embrace Kingdom living, we step into a reality where Heaven's abundance meets Earth's need. We become vessels of His power, carriers of His presence, and agents of His transformation.

Prayer for Kingdom Understanding

THE WORD OF GOD IS THE CORNERSTONE OF KINGDOM LIVING.

Father God, I thank You for revealing Your Kingdom. I pray for wisdom and revelation to understand Your ways and Your Kingdom principles. Lord, help me to see beyond earthly systems and align myself with Your Kingdom culture. Transform my mindset and values to reflect Heaven's perspective. Thank You for making me a citizen of Your Kingdom through Christ Jesus. I receive the authority and privileges that come with this citizenship, and I commit to walking worthy of this high calling. Guide me in representing Your Kingdom well in every area of my life. In Jesus' name. Amen.

CHAPTER TWO

DEVELOPING YOUR CHARACTER THROUGH CHRIST

Character is the foundation of who we are and how we interact with the world around us. But what does it mean to develop character through Christ? This chapter explores the transformative journey of aligning our nature with God's nature. Whether you're new to faith or have walked with God for years, understanding how to cultivate Christ-like character is essential for every believer. We'll examine practical steps and biblical principles that guide us in this lifelong process of transformation.

What is character? The word character is defined in the Oxford Languages as "the mental and moral qualities distinctive to an individual."[1] As human beings, we all have different personalities and character traits. Some may be naturally kind and compassionate, while others struggle with anger or selfishness. Our

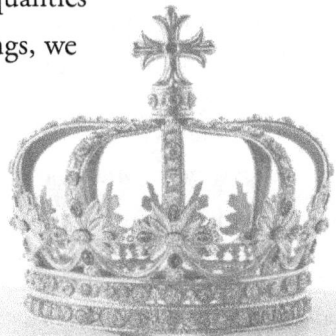

---

1 The language data is provided by Oxford Languages, part of Oxford University Press

character tends to be shaped by our experiences, upbringing, and the people we surround ourselves with. May I suggest a powerful Scripture?

Do not be deceived: "Bad company ruins good morals."
(1 Corinthians 15:33 ESV)

This is huge in the life of a believer. We must watch whom we surround ourselves with. Let me also warn you to be careful whom you go into covenant with. I once heard someone say, "You show me your friends, and I'll show you your future." Think about that!

You may ask, "How do I obtain the character of Christ?"

- Surrendering your old ways of thinking
- Changing your behavior
- Embracing new ways that align with God's Word
- Praying daily
- Reading your daily bread
- Taking intentional time to talk with God
- Increase your faith. Believe even when it looks challenging

Let me explain further. In Kingdom living, you're encouraged to diligently study the Word of God. The Bible is our guide for life, and it contains countless examples of Christ's character traits that we can emulate. By reading and studying the Word, we can learn more about who He is and what it means to be like Him.

Another way to obtain the character of Christ is through prayer. Developing godly character takes effort and sometimes we may struggle in certain areas. Through prayer, we can ask for God's help in developing the specific traits we desire. Also, remaining accountable to godly leadership.

It's important to surround ourselves with people who can encourage us and help us grow in our faith. This includes finding a church community where we can learn from others, receive guidance, and be held accountable for our character development.

Then, as new creations in Christ Jesus, He becomes our ultimate role model for growth and development.

> For to this you were called, because Christ also suffered for us, leaving us an example, that you should follow His steps (1 Peter 2:21 NKJV)

Simply stated, Christ is the example of our faith. Faith increases one day at a time. Faith in Greek is the word *pistis* which has to do with God's divine persuasion. Being distinct from human belief yet involving it. Faith is a gift from God to believe, trust, and take confidence in Him which is instilled within the yielded believer so they can know what God prefers according to the revelation of Scripture. Have you been tried in your faith? Most people have. Some have been waiting on a miracle, a spouse, a house, a child, an increase in your finances, or a healing with a health condition... for life happens at a moment's notice to cause us to waiver in our faith. I submit to you that faith is the force to change your reality. We believe in the God of the Bible. In the moments when our faith is on trial continue to stand on the Word of God which is the final authority in all matters. His words are our faith. I encourage you, when challenged with faith, to watch your words, for your words have power. Speak and believe in faith. Faith is simply believing that it is so. Jesus is our example.

TO WATCH YOUR WORDS, FOR YOUR WORDS HAVE POWER.

The Fruit of the Spirit

The development of Christ-like character flows naturally from the work of the Holy Spirit in our lives. As we submit to His transforming power, we begin to manifest what Scripture calls "the fruit of the Spirit." The Apostle Paul describes this fruit in his letter to the Galatians:

> But the fruit of the Spirit is love, joy, peace, longsuffering, kindness, goodness, faithfulness, gentleness, self-control.
> (Galatians 5:22-23 NKJV)

This fruit isn't something we manufacture through self-effort. Rather, it grows naturally as we abide in Christ. Just as a healthy apple tree naturally produces apples, a life connected to Christ naturally produces godly character. Let's explore each aspect of this spiritual fruit and how it shapes our character.

Love forms the foundation of Christ-like character. This *agape* love we defined in Chapter 1 flows from God Himself. It enables us to love others sacrificially, even when they don't deserve it. This love transforms how we view others and motivates our actions toward them.

A LIFE CONNECTED TO CHRIST NATURALLY PRODUCES GODLY CHARACTER.

Joy follows as a natural expression of God's life within us. Unlike happiness, which depends on circumstances, spiritual joy remains steady through life's ups and downs. It springs from our relationship with Christ and our understanding of His faithfulness, giving us strength even in difficult times.

Peace that surpasses understanding becomes our portion, calming our hearts and minds regardless of external circumstances. This peace isn't just the absence of conflict but the presence of God's tranquility in our lives. It enables us to maintain composure and trust in God's control even amid chaos.

Longsuffering, or patience, develops as we learn to trust God's timing. This quality helps us endure difficulties without becoming bitter or giving up. It reflects Christ's patient nature and helps us maintain stability in challenging relationships and circumstances.

Kindness and goodness reflect God's heart toward others. These qualities move us beyond mere politeness to genuine care for others' well-being. They lead us to practical acts of service and compassion, showing Christ's character in tangible ways.

Faithfulness grows as we learn to be dependable and trustworthy, just as God is faithful to us. This quality touches every area of life—our relationships, responsibilities, and commitments. It builds trust and opens doors for greater influence.

Gentleness balances strength with sensitivity. This isn't weakness, but power under control - the same quality Jesus demonstrated in dealing with broken people. It enables us to handle delicate situations and difficult people with wisdom and grace.

Self-control rounds out the fruit, enabling us to master our impulses and emotions. This quality helps us choose right actions regardless of feelings or circumstances. It's particularly crucial in today's world of instant gratification and moral compromise.

We Must Cooperate

These qualities don't develop overnight or in isolation. They grow together as different aspects of Christ's character formed in us. The process requires both divine grace and our cooperation. Here's how we can participate in this character development:

First, we must stay connected to Christ through regular prayer and Bible study. Just as a branch must stay connected to the vine to bear fruit, we must maintain our connection to Christ to develop His character. This means creating daily habits of spiritual nourishment.

Second, we need to respond promptly to the Holy Spirit's conviction. When He points out areas needing change, immediate obedience accelerates character growth. Delayed obedience often leads to missed opportunities for development.

REMEMBER THAT CHARACTER DEVELOPMENT IS A LIFELONG JOURNEY.

Third, we must embrace the challenges that test and strengthen character. Difficulties aren't obstacles to character development—they're opportunities for growth. Each challenge presents a chance to exercise and strengthen godly qualities.

Regular self-examination also plays a vital role. We should periodically ask ourselves questions like: "Am I becoming more patient? More loving? More self-controlled?" This isn't to condemn ourselves but to identify areas needing growth and celebrate progress made.

Community support strengthens character development. We need relationships with other believers who can encourage us, hold us accountable, and provide examples of Christ-like character. These connections help us stay on track and provide practical wisdom for growth.

Remember that character development is a lifelong journey. Some days will show clear progress, while others may reveal how far we have to go. The key is maintaining our focus on Christ and allowing His Spirit to continue His transforming work in us.

Christlikeness

Jesus lived a sinless life on Earth while demonstrating all of these characteristics. The Bible teaches that Jesus was tempted at all points, facing various trials and tribulations. Jesus is our example of being tried by evil to prove His character and the steadfastness of His faith in God. He is our perfect sacrifice.

> For we have not a high priest which cannot be touched with
> the feeling of our infirmities; but was in all points tempted
> like as we are, yet without sin. (Hebrews 4:15 NKJV)

Jesus was steadfast in His faith and obedience to God. By studying His life through the Word of God and following His teachings, we can learn to develop a strong character in and through Him.

What is transformation? Transformation is a thorough or dramatic change in form or appearance. In his writings to the church of Ephesus, Apostle Paul describes this process. He describes a person who goes from being "dead in trespasses and sins," meaning one who commits an offense even against Judaic law, to being saved by the grace of God according to one's faith in Christ.

> And you He made alive, who were dead in trespasses and
> sins, in which you once walked according to the course
> of this world, according to the prince of the power of the
> air, the spirit who now works in the sons of disobedience,
> among whom also we all once conducted ourselves in the
> lusts of our flesh, fulfilling the desires of the flesh and the
> mind, and were by nature children of wrath, just as the
> others. (Ephesians 2:1-3 NKJV)

What is Paul saying? He states that we have all known the difference between right and wrong, beginning from a very early age, and we have found ourselves to be disobedient. No one has ever been perfect. A man of God I admire used to say, "We're imperfect people serving a perfect God." Doing those things that displease God is characterized by the part of man who is un-renewed in mind and without covenant with God in Christ Jesus. As a result, we "were" dead in trespasses and sins.

"WE'RE IMPERFECT PEOPLE SERVING A PERFECT GOD."

Willful Unbelief

Apostle Paul is saying that this is due to the influences of the prince of the power of the air, which is Satan, himself. The Bible describes his influence as such that works in the sons of disobedience. Disobedience is an interesting word. Disobedience here in the context of Scripture has to do with willful unbelief, the refusal to be convinced by God's voice. In man's decision to reject God's offers of faith, disobedience is the refusal to be persuaded in the heart concerning obeying His will (Word).

Disobedience is one way of describing what occurred in the Garden of Eden (in the beginning), but I'd prefer to use the term "willful unbelief." Now, before I go any further, I would encourage you to go back and read Genesis Chapters 1 through 3. Specifically, Chapters 1 and 2 so that you can better understand God's original intent for man. Genesis Chapter 3 leads us into the subtle deception of the serpent.

One of the things I've learned over the years is that growing up in church, hearing about Jesus, and even reading some Scripture, I wasn't necessarily able to comprehend on a level that I would be able to internalize the experiences of God's Word and apply them to my life back then. So, I was taught to love God and believe in Christ Jesus, but I didn't have any revelation of His Word.

My parents took me and my siblings to church, including Sunday School, every weekend. I tell my mother all the time that I never appreciated those wool suits she'd make me wear. Can anyone relate? We stayed in church most of the day. We went to the local buffet for dinner after morning and afternoon worship and went back to church Sunday night for Young People Willing Workers (YPWW). Sundays were typically a full day dedicated to the Lord. We'd go to Bible study during the week, but I was a drummer. So, I participated on the Praise and Worship team on both Wednesday evenings and Sunday services. Playing the drums is where I gained my appreciation for the anointing.

So, like many of you, I didn't have professional lessons. I learned to play the drums by beating on pots and pans using kitchen ladles during family get-togethers as a toddler. God anointed me to play! But I digress: fast-forwarding to the understanding at hand regarding the distinction between the term's disobedience versus willful unbelief.

You may ask, why not disobedience? I prefer not to use the term disobedience because there's nowhere in Scripture where it says that Adam and Eve were disobedient. Adam and Eve did not listen. They failed to uphold what was instructed to them. The Scriptures teach us that Adam and Eve simply didn't believe in God as it relates to what God told Adam. "Willful unbelief" began when Adam and Eve ate the forbidden fruit in the Garden of Eden. God had created a perfect environment for them. If you recall, the Bible tells us that everything God made was good, yet we understand that Adam and Eve did have the ability not to believe God.

Separated from the Father

Let's look closely at Scripture for clarity. Here's what God tells Adam:

> And the Lord God commanded the man, saying, "Of every tree of the garden you may freely eat; but of the tree of the knowledge of good and evil you shall not eat, for in the day that you eat of it you shall surely die."
>
> (Genesis 2:16-17 NKJV)

He wanted their love and honor for Him to be a free choice. Yet, the punishment for their "willful unbelief" was tremendous, and its effects reached far beyond that moment. Their bodies and souls were corrupted, and they were separated from God—the only source of life.

I'd like to speak about being separated from the Father for a moment. Specifically, when the Bible says that "in the day that you eat of it you shall surely die," we understand that God was not referring to a physical death or separation but one that is spiritual. The spiritual death that Adam and Eve would experience would be a separation from the goodness, fellowship, resource, and dominion of the Father. Here's the kicker: Adam and Eve listened to the enemy. NO! Believers, don't allow the enemy to trick you. When you know what God has said to you, stand on the Word. Don't deviate from God's Word. It is all a smokescreen to get you off track and lead you to a path of death and destruction. Be watchful. Pray. Be alert. The enemy is deceptive, a trickster.

Since the day Adam ate the forbidden fruit, the whole world has been affected by Adam's decision, resulting in all future generations inheriting his sinful nature until the restoration of all things by Christ Jesus. Apostle Paul goes on to tell us that in the fallen state of man, we "once" lived according to the course of the world or age, meaning we all have once lived outside the ways, the will, and the plan of God for our lives. I am so grateful for the grace of God. Aren't you grateful that His grace covers us? The grace of God is favor and protection.

Ephesians 2:1 the Bible says, "He made alive." I want you to notice that "He made alive" is italicized in Scripture, which tells us that it was not a part of the original translation but was added to provide clarity in English by the translators.

It is critical to understand that you and I have been "made alive" in Christ Jesus, meaning that we are now empowered with divine life. You've been infused with eternal life through faith in Christ Jesus and the receiving of His shed blood for all your trespasses and sins. You are a new creation in Christ.

> Therefore, if anyone *is* in Christ, *he is* a new creation; old things have passed away; behold, all things have become new. (2 Corinthians 5:17)

The word "new" here is the Greek word *kairos,* which means new in quality or innovation. It also means to be fresh in development or opportunity because you have never been like this before. You have been predestined for a new experience with God. Welcome to the Kingdom of God!

As our character aligns with Christ's, we begin to grasp the depths of His salvation. Chapter 3 will reveal how this salvation transforms every aspect of our lives, making us entirely new creations in Christ.

Prayer to Build Your Character in Christ

Father, I pray that I am being transformed into the image of Your dear Son. I am being transformed into a new person by changing the way I think and respond to my circumstances. I thank You for being the God who humbles me and has given me a repenting heart. I thank You, God, for removing the pride that keeps me from seeing myself as You see me. Today, I receive that my heart is filled with a spirit of jubilation, songs of praise, and gratitude to my Lord and Savior. In Jesus' name. Amen.

CHAPTER THREE

UNDERSTANDING GOD'S SALVATION

Salvation forms the very foundation and heartbeat of the Christian faith, yet its depths and implications often exceed our initial understanding. The word salvation in Greek is soteria, which means deliverance, preservation, and safety. It represents far more than just a ticket to Heaven—it embodies God's comprehensive plan for humanity's redemption and restoration.

I submit that understanding salvation is essential for every believer. In this chapter, we'll explore what it means to be saved, why we need salvation, and how this divine gift transforms every aspect of our lives. By examining key Scriptures and practical applications, you'll gain a deeper appreciation for this magnificent gift that Christ purchased with His own blood.

When Jesus declared, "I have come that they may have life, and that they may have it more abundantly" (John 10:10), He was speaking of the transformative power of salvation. The

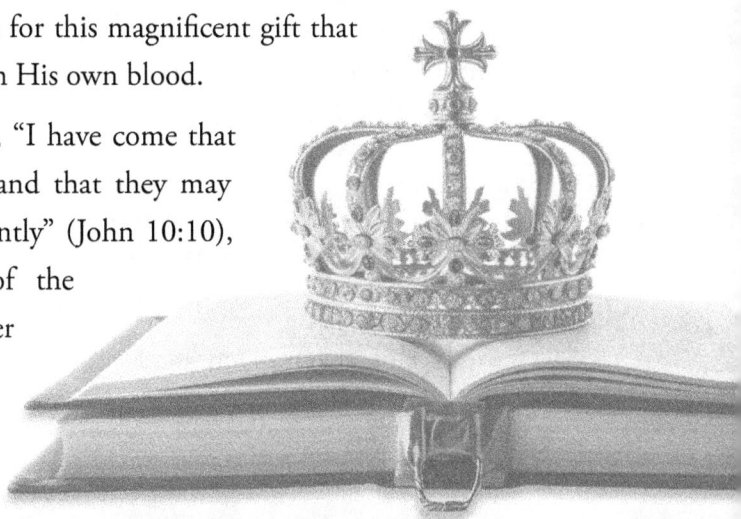

word "life" here is the Greek word zoe, which refers to the very life of God Himself. Through salvation, we receive not just forgiveness but the very nature of God implanted within us.

Salvation is one of the most essential and fundamental concepts in Christianity. It is often referred to as "God's plan" or "God's gift" for humanity. But what exactly is salvation? And why do Christians believe it is necessary? Let's look at the Word of God.

> For God so loved the world that He gave His only begotten Son, that whoever believes in Him should not perish but have everlasting life. For God did not send His Son into the world to condemn the world, but that the world through Him might be saved. (John 3:16-17 NKJV)

What we find are two key principles to the finished work of Jesus: salvation and everlasting life. Salvation refers to the deliverance of humanity from sin and its consequences, leading to eternal life with God. As the Scripture teaches us, this occurs according to our belief and faith in Him (Christ). I want you to notice that Christ did not come to "condemn the world" but rather to save the world. If we take a closer look at this, there is a great revelation. Jesus tells us in John 3:17 that he did not come to condemn. The word condemn here is the Greek word *krino,* which means to judge, and come to a choice (decision, judgment) either positive or negative. Let's look into some dimensions of salvation according to this great gospel.

Justification, Sanctification, and Glorification

The dimensions of salvation extend far beyond the initial moment of accepting Christ. While that moment marks our entrance into God's family, salvation encompasses past, present, and future aspects that touch every area of our lives. Understanding these dimensions helps us grasp the fullness of what Christ accomplished for us.

1. Justification: Forgiven by the judge – Imagine you've been brought before a judge because of a massive debt you could never repay. Instead of punishment, the judge forgives your debt entirely and declares you innocent. This act of forgiveness isn't something you earned—it's a gift. Scripture declares, "Therefore, having been justified by faith, we have peace with God through our Lord Jesus Christ" (Romans 5:1). Justification is the moment we are forgiven by God, declared righteous, and reconciled to Him because of Jesus' sacrifice. It is the beginning of our salvation journey. Through Christ's sacrifice, God declares us righteous, completely forgiven and fully accepted. This isn't based on our performance but solely on Christ's finished work. The moment we believe, God credits Christ's righteousness to our account. We stand before Him as if we had never sinned, clothed in Christ's perfect righteousness.

2. Sanctification: Learning to live in freedom – Now imagine being released from prison after your debt is forgiven. You're free, but you must learn how to live outside the prison walls—how to embrace a new way of life, leaving old habits behind as Scripture instructs: "But now that you have been set free from sin and have become slaves of God, the benefit you reap leads to holiness, and the result is eternal life" (Romans 6:22). Sanctification is the ongoing process of God shaping us into the likeness of Christ. It requires effort on our part, such as prayer, Bible study, and living in obedience, but it is powered by the Holy Spirit. This is the daily process of becoming more like Christ in

our thoughts, attitudes, and actions. The Holy Spirit works within us, transforming our character and empowering us to live holy lives. This isn't about earning God's favor—we already have that through justification. Rather, it's about growing into the new identity He's given us.

3. Glorification: Living in perfect freedom – Finally, imagine a future where you live in perfect freedom—a world where all the struggles and imperfections of life are gone. This is the ultimate restoration, where you experience the fullness of life as it was meant to be. The Apostle Paul instructs, "For I consider that the sufferings of this present time are not worth comparing with the glory that is to be revealed to us" (Romans 8:18). Glorification is the future promise of eternal life with God, where we will receive glorified bodies and live in perfect harmony with Him. When Christ returns, we'll receive glorified bodies free from sin's presence and effects. This final stage completes our salvation, fully realizing our adoption as God's children. While we taste aspects of this now, its full manifestation awaits Christ's return.

Understanding salvation's full scope changes how we live today. We don't work to earn God's approval—we already have it in Christ. Instead, we learn to live from the victory Christ has already won. This truth frees us from performance-based religion and launches us into relationship-based living.

Salvation also transforms our identity. We're no longer defined by our past failures or present struggles but by our position in Christ. We are new creations, completely forgiven, fully accepted, and eternally secure. This new identity becomes the foundation for all growth and transformation.

The Security of Our Salvation

The security of our salvation rests not on our ability to maintain it but on Christ's finished work and God's faithfulness. Just as we couldn't earn salvation through good works, we can't lose it through poor performance. God's grace, which saved us initially, continues to keep us secure in Christ.

This security doesn't promote careless living but rather inspires grateful obedience. Understanding the magnitude of what Christ accomplished for us naturally produces a desire to please Him. We serve not out of fear of punishment but out of love and gratitude.

Salvation also places us in a new community—the family of God. We're not saved in isolation but born into a spiritual family. This community provides support, accountability, and opportunities for growth as we journey together toward spiritual maturity.

THIS NEW IDENTITY BECOMES THE FOUNDATION FOR ALL GROWTH AND TRANSFORMATION.

The power of salvation extends beyond personal transformation to impact every relationship and circumstance. It affects how we view ourselves, relate to others, handle difficulties, and approach life's challenges. Through salvation, we gain access to divine resources for every situation we face.

As we grow in understanding salvation's fullness, our faith increases, and our witness strengthens. We begin to see circumstances through Kingdom perspective, knowing that the same power that saved us continues working in us, transforming us increasingly into Christ's image.

Jesus understood his role as our Lord and Savior.

> And if anyone hears My words and does not believe, I do not judge him; for I did not come to judge the world but

to save the world. He who rejects Me, and does not receive My words, has that which judges him—the word that I have spoken will judge him in the last day.

(John 12:47-48 NKJV)

The word judge here in John 12:47-48 is the same Greek word krino, used in John 3:17. I want you to see that Jesus says it will be the word that He spoke that will make the determinations as it relates to our salvation. The Hebrew writer brings even more clarity to the power of the Word of God when he says:

> For the Word of God is living and powerful, and sharper than any two-edged sword, piercing even to the division of soul and spirit, and of joints and marrow, and is a discerner of the thoughts and intents of the heart.

(Hebrews 4:12)

The Word of God discerns our thoughts and intentions. Heart decisions are very important as they relate to our eternal destiny. Watch your heart posture, be careful, and examine it against the Word of God.

> The heart is deceitful above all things and beyond cure. Who can understand it? I the Lord search the heart and examine the mind, to reward each person according to their conduct, according to what their deeds deserve.

(Jeremiah 17:9-10)

Focus on the word "deceitful" in that Scripture: deliberate to cause harm, dishonest, untrustworthy, lies, fraudulent. The power of the Word of God cannot be underestimated. It is a living and powerful force that can pierce through our very being and reveal our true thoughts and intentions. As believers, it is important for us to constantly examine our hearts and align them with the Word of God. This not only ensures our salvation but also guides us in living a life that is pleasing to God by faith.

Notice the distinction here. Jesus said that He has come to save the world not to judge it. If I were to go one step further regarding our salvation, Apostle Peter said something very profound when addressing the Sanhedrin in Jerusalem. Who's the Sanhedrin? The Sanhedrin was a Jewish judicial and legislative assembly that existed in ancient Israel at both the local and central levels. The Greek word for Sanhedrin is the word sunedrion, which means "sitting together." The Sanhedrin was also known for being the supreme council and tribunal of the Jews during post exilic times headed by a High Priest having religious, civil, and criminal jurisdiction.

HE HAS COME TO SAVE THE WORLD NOT TO JUDGE IT.

Jesus was accused of blasphemy, which was a religious offense, meaning he allegedly said something disrespectful to God. In the eyes of the Jewish leaders, when Jesus claimed to be God's son he was insulting God. Apostle Peter says about Jesus being the resurrection from the dead:

> Nor is there salvation in any other, for there is no other name under Heaven given among men by which we must be saved. (Acts 4:12 NKJV)

Apostle Peter points them to the finished work of Jesus Christ, which is essential because we are born into sin and condemned to God's judgment.

The Bible teaches us that the law was given as a tutor to bring us to Christ so that we may be justified by faith.

Apostle Paul gives us further revelation into salvation in his writings to the church of Ephesus.

> For by grace, you have been saved through faith, and that not of yourselves; it is the gift of God, not of works, lest anyone should boast. (Ephesians 2:8-9 NKJV)

Earlier, I mentioned that "saved" is the Latin word salvare. But the word "saved" is also the Greek word sozo, which means to be healed, preserved, rescued or God rescuing the believer from the penalty and power of sin. Sozo is the root of Soter or Soteria, which is translated as "salvation." So, salvation is the work of Christ, which you receive by faith according to grace, being delivered from error, fault, and corrupt notions in His (Christ) moral purity and His (Christ) reconciliation.

Apostle Paul grants us plenty of examples of the work of salvation in Christ Jesus. Apostle Paul writes to Titus, who was an early church leader, a trusted companion of the Apostle and a faithful servant of the Lord. Paul states:

> But according to His mercy He saved us, through the washing of regeneration and renewing of the Holy Spirit, whom He poured out on us abundantly through Jesus Christ our Savior. (Titus 3:5-6 NKJV)

God displayed His love by sending His Son, Jesus Christ, to die on the Cross for our sins. Because of Christ, we can come to God by faith. We can do nothing to earn salvation; it is the gift of God according to the

Word of the Lord. We must believe that Jesus Christ is risen from the dead, and ask Him to forgive, save us, and come into our lives. He is our final payment for sin. We must believe in Jesus Christ and claim His promise of eternal life.

We will further clarify eternal life in several chapters from now, which Jesus gives us for believing in Him. A key component of our salvation is faith. We discussed faith above. Faith is vital in the life of a believer. I want to speak to faith more succinctly. Faith is the Greek word *pistis* which we stated earlier having to do with confidence and trust in God to believe His Word that Jesus is the Son of God and through Him we are saved.

Bringing more insight here would be to say, it's not just your and my believing or having faith in God regarding Christ and his death on the cross because we know that Christ is no longer there. We understand that Christ has risen from the dead and is now seated on the right hand of the majesty from on High, our Father.

In Apostle Paul's first letter to the church of Corinth, he speaks of faith in the resurrection.

> And if Christ is not risen, then our preaching is empty, and your faith is also empty. Yes, and we are found false witnesses of God because we have testified of God that He raised up Christ, whom He did not raise up—if in fact the dead do not rise. (1 Corinthians 15:14-15)

The resurrection of Christ Jesus from the dead is the reality of our faith. You and I are to now have faith in his finished work and recognize by the revelation of Scripture that that work is now complete in us, as new creations. In other words, we're talking about Christ's death, crucifixion, burial, resurrection, ascension, and seating and what occurred in you and me throughout this process.

Salvation by faith initiates our journey of transformation, making us new creations in Christ Jesus. In Chapter 4, we'll discover what this new creation reality means and how it fundamentally changes who we are.

Prayer of Salvation

Father, I repent of my sins and surrender my life. I thank You for cleansing and washing me by the blood of Jesus. Jesus Christ is the Son of God. He died on the cross for my sins and rose again on the third day with all power in His hand. I receive that in Christ I have the victory. I believe this in my heart unto righteousness and I confess with my mouth unto my salvation. Lord, Your Word say that you'd never make me ashamed. Lord, Your Word says that whosoever shall call upon the name of the Lord shall be saved. Today, I'm saved, I'm sanctified and filled with the Holy Spirit. Father, thank You for it now. I receive it by faith, in Jesus' name. Amen.

CHAPTER FOUR

NEW CREATION
IN CHRIST JESUS

The concept of becoming a "new creation" stands as one of the most profound promises in Scripture. Far more than self-improvement or behavioral modification, this divine transformation fundamentally changes who we are at our core. In this chapter, we'll explore what it means to be made new in Christ, examining how this spiritual reality manifests in our daily lives. Whether you've just begun your faith journey or have walked with Christ for years, understanding your identity as a new creation opens doors to living in the fullness God intends.

What is a new creation in Christ Jesus? Let's begin with the Scripture.

> Therefore, if anyone *is* in Christ, *he is* a new creation; old things have passed away; behold, all things have become new. (2 Corinthians 5:17 NKJV)

Embrace your new life as a new creation in Christ, where you're immersed in the transformative

power of God's love and grace. As you understand and embrace your identity in Him, you'll experience the fullness of His anointing and the potential for positive change in your life through faith.

> Buried with Him in baptism, in which you also were raised with *Him* through faith in the working of God, who raised Him from the dead. (Colossians 2:12 NKJV)

As a new creation in Christ Jesus, you are also immersed in the revelation of being received by God according to the finished work of Jesus, meaning you are now one with the Father through Christ and what He accomplished for you on the cross. By His finished work, you have been made new. The word "new" is interesting as it has several meanings. In Hebrew, it's *neos,* which means something that has never happened before. In Greek, "new" is the word *kainos,* which means new quality or new ways. So, if the Scripture tells us that in Christ we are "new creations" and Adam was the original man or original creation, then what the Word of God is telling us is that we must be something other than the original man. Why? Because we are new in the anointing.

You are now indwelled by the Holy Spirit. In Christ, even the old things are passed away, and not just sins but old ways of thinking and old ways of doing things are passed away. As a new creation in Christ, God gives new thoughts, new strategies, new vision, new insights, and new levels of creativity. The Scripture tells us in 2 Corinthians 5:17 that "behold, all things are become new," meaning that you see this as a reality of the new creation by faith. As you behold or see through the eyes of faith through the finished work of Jesus, you will see things transforming in your life.

The Transformation Business

Jesus, in the person of the Holy Spirit, is in the transformation business for all who believe in His name. He is transforming people like me and like you through the ministry of the Holy Spirit daily.

Second Corinthians says something profound. I pray it blesses you:

> But we all, with unveiled face, beholding as in a mirror the glory of the Lord, are being transformed into the same image from glory to glory, just as by the Spirit of the Lord.
> (2 Corinthians 3:18 NKJV)

Transformed here is the Greek word *metamorphoo,* where we get the English terms metamorphosis and metamorphize. Transformed means to be changed after being with or changing form in keeping with inner reality. You are being transformed from the inside out. When the Spirit of God transforms you, you become a new creation in Christ Jesus. This process was completed for you at the cross and in the resurrection.

YOU ARE BEING TRANSFORMED FROM THE INSIDE OUT.

Prophet Isaiah declared in Isaiah 53:10, "He shall see His seed, He shall prolong His days." In other words, the work was finished at the cross on Calvary. When Jesus Christ rose from the dead on the third day according to the Word of God, you and I rose with Him a new creation in Christ Jesus. As a new creation in Christ Jesus, you have been given a new identity and purpose. You are no longer bound by your past mistakes or failures, but you are now clothed with the righteousness of Christ. This means that your worth is not determined by your actions or accomplishments but by the love and grace of God.

Your purpose as a new creation is to reflect the image of Christ to the world around you. Through the power of the Holy Spirit working in you, you are being transformed into His likeness and glory. Your life should be a testimony to others of God's love, forgiveness, and transformative power. Remember, you are a citizen of the Kingdom. You represent Jesus Christ. What an honor it is to show the world the great God whom you serve.

Let's look even further into God's transformative ability. We know that Christ lived the perfect Christian life. The Bible is very clear about this.

> For He made Him who knew no sin *to be* sin for us, that
> we might become the righteousness of God in Him.
>
> (2 Corinthians 5:21 NKJV)

This is the light and revelation that births transformation by the Holy Spirit. In other words, because of what Jesus completed in His life on Earth through His crucifixion, death, burial, resurrection, ascension, and seating, He now lives through every child of God who believes in Him. Jesus Christ wants to live His life in and through you.

The Mercy Seat

I was meditating on the Word of God, and the Holy Spirit said to me, "Christ living through the believer is the love of God," then He took me to this Scripture:

> In this the love of God was manifested toward us, that
> God has sent His only begotten Son into the world, that
> we might live through Him. In this is love, not that we

loved God, but that He loved us and sent His Son to be the propitiation for our sins. (I John 4:9-10 NKJV)

Propitiation is an old English term that means the mercy seat. The mercy seat is the Greek word hilasterion, which means that which makes expiation or propitiation. In the Old Covenant, in the most holy place or the place where God dwells, there was the Ark of the Covenant, and above the ark was a gold lid or the mercy seat, a chair upon which no one sat. The mercy seat was protected by two cherubim on both sides. But now that the work is finished, Jesus has taken his rightful seat.

Through His sacrifice on the cross, Jesus became the ultimate mercy seat for all of humanity. He took our sins upon Himself and, through His death and resurrection, made a way for us to be reconciled with God. This act of love and grace allows Christ to live through us as believers.

What a wonderful thing it is to know that we have hope in Jesus Christ and an eternal home in Heaven! It's even more glorious to know that He lives in you and is with you in the person of the Holy Spirit. You're not a sinner saved by grace. Friends of God, you are saved by faith through the grace of God in Christ Jesus. Hallelujah, you're in the family of God. Welcome to the Kingdom!!

You Must Be Born Again

I'd like to bring you further into the truth of the new creation reality by expounding on what it means to be born again. As a part of the revelation of becoming a new creation, the Bible teaches us that we must be born again. In the born-again process, when you receive salvation, one of the things you discover is that Jesus Christ was raised from the dead for your and my justification. What's Justification? It's the Greek word *dikaiosis*, which means to be acquitted, the process of absolution or Christ's full payment of the debt for sin liberating the believer from all divine condemnation. When the Father sees you, He sees you "as if" you never sinned. He no longer sees you in a fallen state; He sees the finished work of His Son, Jesus Christ in you.

Taking a closer look at what it means to be born again. Being "born again" means "from above, from Heaven, from the beginning or anew." What Jesus was saying in His conversation with Nicodemus was that you must be "born from above." You must receive that you came out of God in the new birth by faith in Christ Jesus. By the shed blood of Jesus, your sins have been taken away. Today, as a new creation in Christ Jesus, you walk in this understanding of salvation by receiving what Christ did for you in His death, crucifixion, burial, resurrection, ascension, and seating. Some people ask the question, are you a born-again Christian? I submit to you that there's only one Christian, and that's a born-again Christian.

WHEN THE FATHER SEES YOU, HE SEES YOU "AS IF" YOU NEVER SINNED.

Jesus, in His encounter with Nicodemus in John Chapter 3, said that Nicodemus must be born again.

> Jesus answered and said to him, Most assuredly, I say to you, unless one is born again, he cannot see the Kingdom of God. (John 3:3 NKJV)

Jesus told Nicodemus that unless he was born again, he couldn't see the Kingdom of God, meaning Nicodemus must believe in Christ as the Messiah and his Lord and Savior, or else he couldn't see the Kingdom of God.

To see the Kingdom of God means that you have understood that you can now live by Kingdom principles. To see the Kingdom of God means you now know that there's a better way to live because of your covenant relationship with Christ. Jesus goes on to tell Nicodemus, the Rabbi, that it is important not only to see the Kingdom of God but also to enter the Kingdom of God. Jesus tells him that one must be born of water and the Spirit to enter.

> Jesus answered, "Most assuredly, I say to you unless one is born of water and the Spirit, he cannot enter the Kingdom of God. (John 3:5 NKJV)

In other words, there is the baptism with water or the natural birth that Nicodemus experienced, and then there is the process of being born of the Spirit, meaning that Christ now lives in you in the person of the Holy Spirit because you are a receiver of Christ's price of redemption. Together, you come into the reality of the "new birth," and you are now empowered to see and enter the Kingdom of God by faith.

The born-again experience is the rebirth of the human spirit in connection with God.

> Having been born again, not of corruptible seed but incorruptible, through the Word of God which lives and abides forever. (I Peter 1:24 NKJV)

Apostle Peter gives us insight into the born-again experience as well, with the understanding that the other way to be born again is through the Word of God. The Bible teaches us that the seed is the Word of God (Mark 4:20). The Word of God is living and abiding, and through the preaching of the gospel, the believer is begotten to newness of being. Natural birth is understood as what results in decay and death, but in the new birth, the seed remains in him, and he cannot sin because he is born of God (I John 3:9).

Created and Formed

The understanding of being born again by the incorruptible seed of the Word of God can be traced back to the beginning when God created and formed man, according to Genesis Chapters 1 and 2. I encourage you to read these chapters; what you'll find is God's original intent for man. God created man in His own image and likeness, He then put the spirit of life in him.

> Then God said, Let Us make man in Our image, according to Our likeness; let them have dominion over the fish of the sea, over the birds of the air, and over the cattle, over all the earth and over every creeping thing that creeps on the earth. So, God created man in His *own* image; in the image of God, He created him; male and female He created them. (Genesis 1:26-27 NKJV)

The breath that was breathed into the nostrils of Adam by God was a connection to eternity. This was pre-fall man.

> And the Lord God formed man of the dust of the ground, and breathed into his nostrils the breath of life, and man became a living being. (Genesis 2:7 NKJV)

The revelation of this Scripture is this: before man became a living being, he had animation, according to Genesis 1:26-27. Why? He was created but not yet formed, as he (Adam) was in God. Let me further explain.

In Genesis 1:27, the word created is used three times. But in Genesis 2:7, the word formed is used. When you read Genesis Chapter 1, the writer talks of how God said, "Let there be" throughout the first chapter, and in verse twenty-seven, God said, "So God **created** man in His own image…" But, in Genesis 2:7, God said He **formed** man of the dust of the ground.

The reality is that there is a difference between something being created and something being formed. Created is the Hebrew word *bara,* which means to shape, to bring into existence from nothing. The word "formed" is the Hebrew word *yatsar,* which means to form the thing out of pre-existing material. The Eternal Creator created man in Genesis Chapter 1 out of Himself and then formed man from the dust of the ground, breathing life into him by which man is now alive.

God is the giver and creator of life. When man becomes a living being, he now has life in him. Man's mind, will, emotion, and attitude are to function in line with the Creator who made him. Man has animation before man has life. I really want you to understand this revelation. This is important. Life is not an activity; in other words, man can walk and talk but can also be separated from the life of God; this is why man must be born again.

I would like to go a step further. The Scripture teaches the following.

> But of the tree of the knowledge of good and evil you shall not eat, for **in the day** that you eat of it you shall surely die. (Genesis 2:17 NKJV)

In other words, when Man is in relation with God, he's in one day, but when he is out of alignment with God, he's in another day. When you are born again, you are living "in the day" in Christ Jesus in comparison to those who are not in Christ.

The Prodigal Son

One other example of being born again would be the parable of the prodigal son.

> Then He said: A certain man had two sons. And the younger of them said to his father, 'Father, give me the portion of goods that falls to me.' So, he divided to them his livelihood. And not many days after, the younger son gathered all together, journeyed to a far country, and there wasted his possessions with prodigal living. (Luke 15:11-13)

If I were to define prodigal living, it would be that the prodigal son was not living the way his father desired. The word "prodigal" in Greek is the word asotos, which means extravagantly wasteful because of loose living.

> But when he had spent all, there arose a severe famine in that land, and he began to be in want. Then he went and joined himself to a citizen of that country, and he sent him into his fields to feed swine. (Luke 15:14-15 NKJV)

When living in a day that is outside the will of God for our lives, it's extremely easy to find ourselves in a very bad circumstance that can lead to self-harm. Here is a Jewish boy in a Gentile land who has now squandered all his possessions and now finds himself living amongst the hogs.

Another Kingdom principle worth mentioning is the importance of being mindful of what or even who we join ourselves to. Just like the prodigal son, when we are living outside of God's will, we tend to make poor choices and surround ourselves with people who may lead us further away from Him. We must be wise in our decisions and always seek God's guidance and direction in our relationships. The Scripture goes on to explain.

> And he would gladly have filled his stomach with the pods
> that the swine ate, and no one gave him anything.
> (Luke 15:16 NKJV)

The prodigal son had reached the lowest of the low. He was so desperate for sustenance that he would have gladly eaten what the pigs were eating. This serves as a powerful reminder to us that when we stray from God's will and live a prodigal life, there will be consequences and struggles that come along with it. Good or bad, there are consequences; therefore, making the best decisions is for our benefit. We may find ourselves in desperate situations where we are seeking temporary fulfillment through material possessions or unhealthy relationships, but these will never satisfy us. God is a genius; He is the only one that can fill the voids in our life.

However, the story of the prodigal son doesn't end here. It is just the beginning of his journey back to his father. The next verses show how he humbly repents and returns to his father, who welcomes him with open arms and celebrates his return. This is a beautiful depiction of God's unconditional love for us and His desire for us to come back to Him, no matter how far we have strayed. He cares about us so much.

OUR HEAVENLY FATHER WILL ALWAYS WELCOME US BACK AND CELEBRATE OUR RETURN.

Know that when you said yes to the will of God you made a step to your new beginning. That's great news.

I can recall the times when I was a new creature in Jesus Christ. I was happy, and I felt refreshed. Nothing could cause me to stray from God. My life became sweeter and sweeter. My heart had a new freedom, and I felt a better zest for life and living. Becoming a citizen protected me.

As new creations in Christ, we must remember that no matter how much we stray from God's will, He is always waiting for us with open arms. We must never be too proud or ashamed to turn back to Him and seek forgiveness. Just like the prodigal son's father, our heavenly Father will always welcome us back and celebrate our return.

> But when he came to himself, he said, 'How many of my father's hired servants have bread enough and to spare, and I perish with hunger! I will arise and go to my father and will say to him, "Father, I have sinned against Heaven and before you, and I am no longer worthy to be called your son. Make me like one of your hired servants.
>
> (Luke 15:17-19 NKJV)

You Are a Son

I want you to notice that he came to himself. What a powerful revelation. He recognized who he was and, as a matter of fact, who his father was. As a Kingdom citizen, you must keep in mind who you are and Whose you are. You are a child of Almighty God. Special. Favored. Covered.

Here's the point that I'm driving home. Like the prodigal son, the Lord knew that you would make some mistakes. He knew you might reach a point where you may be willing to become a servant, lowering your standards to be relieved of the negative situation. But it's important to be reminded that you're a son. In Hebrew, the word son is not gender specific. Son in Hebrew has to do with one with the same nature and character. You're a son of the Highest God. The Bible teaches us that when the father saw his son afar off, having compassion on him, ran to him, fell on his neck, and kissed him. The prodigal son was restored, and the Scripture tells us what his father said to his servants.

> Bring out the best robe and put it on him and put a ring
> on his hand and sandals on his feet. And bring the fatted
> calf here and kill it and let us eat and be merry; for this my
> son was dead and is alive again; he was lost and is found.
> And they began to be merry. (Luke 15:22-24)

The father uses the word dead. Dead here does not refer to physical death but rather to spiritual death, being separated from the goodness, fellowship, dominion, and resources of the Father.

Although there may be times when you fall short of his glory, know that God, our Heavenly Father, always seeks to restore fellowship and draw us closer to Him through the blood of Jesus Christ, who is our Savior. As you move forward in this revelation according to Scripture, I want you to know, once again, that you've been born again, and you are a new creation in Christ Jesus. The life of God dwells in you. The prodigal son, the Scripture said, was dead but now alive again to his father. You have been made alive to God by Christ Jesus and His finished work.

Hallelujah!! You are walking by faith. You are now seeing what natural eyes can't see. You are hearing what natural ears can't hear. You are now born in the right dimension. You're in Christ! Jesus is the way to the Spirit of the living God. Glory to God!!

Being a new creation opens the door to experiencing eternal life—not just as a future promise but as a present reality. Chapter 5 will explore how this eternal life flows through every aspect of our Kingdom citizenship.

New Creation in Christ Jesus Prayer

Father, I am resting in the finished work of Christ. Lord God, what Your Son did on the cross removed the burden of having to depend on my own efforts to succeed. Christ's finished work has made an amazing life available to me that I could never achieve on my own. Thank You, Lord, for the shed blood of Christ. I receive that I have been born again by the incorruptible seed of the Word of God. I receive the work of Christ complete in me. I am a receiver of the Holy Spirit. I receive a fresh impartation of your anointing. I receive it by faith, in Jesus' name. Amen.

CHAPTER FIVE

ETERNAL LIFE

When we hear the phrase "eternal life," our thoughts often jump to a future existence in Heaven. However, Jesus spoke of eternal life as something we can experience now—a quality of life that transcends our natural existence. This chapter delves into the multi-dimensional nature of eternal life, exploring how this divine reality transforms our present while securing our future. Together, we'll discover how to access and live in the power of this unstoppable, unquenchable life that Jesus provides.

By accepting the Lord Jesus Christ as our Lord and Savior, we are saved now and forever! We have God's promises, which are in His Word. The Holy Spirit lives in us, and our new relationship with God gives us the blessed assurance of eternal life in Heaven. The Bible promises that "whosoever believeth in him should not perish but have everlasting life." (John 3:16).

Everlasting life is synonymous with eternal life and the words are interchangeable. The term in the Greek is *aionios zoe,* which means unstoppable life, unquenchable life, or life that cannot be

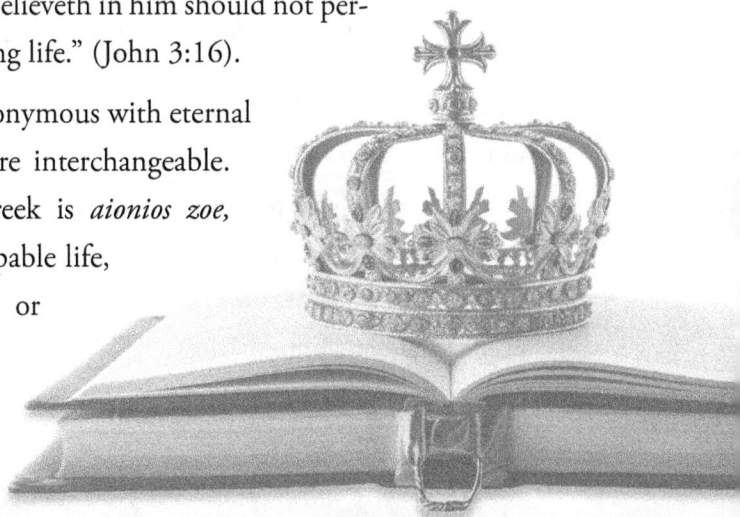

extinguished. Aionios zoe is also understood to mean a quality of life that comes from the Father and not simply quantity as in time. Jesus Christ is eternal life manifested for us.

> And this is the testimony: that God has given us eternal life, and this life is in His Son. He who has the Son has life; he who does not have the Son of God does not have life. (1 John 5:11-12 NKJV)

Once we have received unstoppable or eternal life, we endeavor to learn how to function in it and how to get it working within us. Everything in our lives can be adjusted by eternal life. Understand this: Eternal life is something you have now, not solely when you get to Heaven. It lasts forever because you can't stop it.

In the Word of God, He has given us His mind and principles for us to work with eternal life. Everything God tells us to do is so that eternal life can work at a maximum level. Everything we're instructed to stay away from is so that we can receive eternal life. Every instruction from God is an opportunity to cultivate eternal life and transform our lives for the better. We can tap into the limitless possibilities of eternal life and avoid anything that hinders it.

EVERYTHING IN OUR LIVES CAN BE ADJUSTED BY ETERNAL LIFE.

> And as Moses lifted up the serpent in the wilderness, even so must the Son of Man be lifted up, that whoever believes in Him should not perish but have eternal life. For God so loved the world that He gave His only begotten Son, that whoever believes in Him should not perish but have everlasting life. (John 3:14-16 NKJV)

The Lord Jesus compares Him being lifted or crucified on the cross to Moses lifting the serpent in the wilderness.

> Then, the Lord said to Moses, "Make a fiery serpent, and set it on a pole; and it shall be that everyone who is bitten, when he looks at it, shall live." So, Moses made a bronze serpent, and put it on a pole; and so, it was, if a serpent had bitten anyone, when he looked at the bronze serpent, he lived. (Numbers 21:8-9 NKJV)

God instructed Moses to make a bronze serpent and put it on a pole for all to see. When anyone bitten by a venomous snake looked at the serpent, they were healed, and their lives were saved. This is a foreshadowing of Jesus being lifted on the cross for our sins. When we look to Him in faith, we receive eternal life. Don't you desire to have this eternal life, my friends? The joy, peace, and security are truly remarkable.

We must continue to hold fast to this truth and live according to the principles given in His Word so that eternal life can continue working within us. It's not enough just to receive it; we must also cultivate and nourish it in our lives. This means living a life of obedience and righteousness, staying away from things that can hinder our relationship with God.

Everlasting life is a gift from God. It must be received, not earned, or achieved through good works. Our faith in Jesus Christ and His sacrifice on the cross saves us from our sins and grants us eternal life with God.

In Your Personal Life

- Supernatural peace amid chaos
- Divine wisdom for decisions

- Healing and restoration
- Spiritual discernment

In Relationships

- Unconditional love
- Forgiveness beyond human capacity
- Redemptive influence
- Kingdom impact

In Ministry

- Supernatural authority
- Miraculous provision
- Divine protection
- Kingdom expansion

Kill. Steal. Destroy

Jesus declared in John 10:10, "The thief does not come except to steal, and to kill, and to destroy. I (Jesus) have come that they may have life and have it more abundantly." Abundant life is a choice. This Scripture gives us insight into the enemy's agenda. So, we are aware. Now, we have the information to defeat him.

Beware of the thief, someone who takes without permission as if he has the right to do so. Not so! You have been given authority to defeat his wicked devices and schemes. Here is the power punch: the agenda of the enemy will never change. It will remain the same.

YOU HAVE BEEN GIVEN AUTHORITY TO DEFEAT HIS WICKED DEVICES AND SCHEMES.

Can you recall the times the enemy was determined to destroy you? Do you remember how you felt? Now, recall the time you were determined not to give in to the enemy's devices. A thief will take from you when you least expect it. He's sly and clever. This is why it is vitally important to stay armed and dangerous through the Word of God. The Word of God gives you all the information and strategic insight you need to fight and win. We don't fight the enemy as the world; we fight the enemy with Kingdom principles: prayer, praise, worship, wisdom, fasting, and the words we speak out of our mouths. Affirmations of grace and power are our power.

Don't be deceived! Stay woke. Stay alert.

Listen and understand. If something is attempting to kill, steal, or destroy you in ANY area of your life, such as your relationship with God, your well-being, your faith, your finances, or your health, not only is it not the Spirit of God, but what the Word of the Lord is declaring is that whoever believes in what Christ accomplished on the cross will have the authority to stop it. You have the power to stop the perishing. Why? Because you believe! But don't stop there; I want you to understand that your belief is also about you HAVING something.

The Scripture says that "whoever believes in Him should not perish but have everlasting life." I need you to declare that you have everlasting life. God sent His Son to bring life and abundance to those who believe in Him. This means that, as believers, we have the authority to stop anything causing destruction or harm in our lives. We have been given eternal life, which not only guarantees us a place in Heaven but also empowers us to live victoriously on Earth. With eternal life flowing in us, we're ready to take our first public step of Kingdom citizenship through water baptism. Chapter 6 will guide us through this significant milestone in our faith journey.

Prayer of Eternal Life

Dear Father, thank you for Eternal Life with you. I thank you for causing me to triumph and live a prosperous life. I will not be tricked or discounted by the enemy. In you, I live, move, and have my being. Father, I thank you for seeing me and you desire that I live a life that is courageous in You. I declare that I am a citizen of your Kingdom. By faith, I am victorious. In Jesus' name. Amen.

CHAPTER SIX

BAPTISM: TAKE
THE FIRST STEP

B aptism represents more than a religious ritual or church tradition—
it's a powerful act of identification with Christ's death, burial, and
resurrection. In this chapter, we'll explore the profound significance of
this sacred ordinance and why Jesus commanded all believers to participate in it. Whether you're considering baptism or seeking to understand
its deeper meaning, this chapter will illuminate the transformative power
of this crucial step of obedience.

Don't you agree that it's time we brought baptism back to the forefront
of our faith? This is on my heart. It's been far too long since I've read a
strategic book or heard a detailed message that truly
emphasizes the power of this transformative act. I
pray that this chapter helps you understand
the dynamics and importance of baptism.

While baptism is not required for salvation, it is an important step of obedience
to Christ. You may ask
why it is not required.
Let's investigate
this principle.

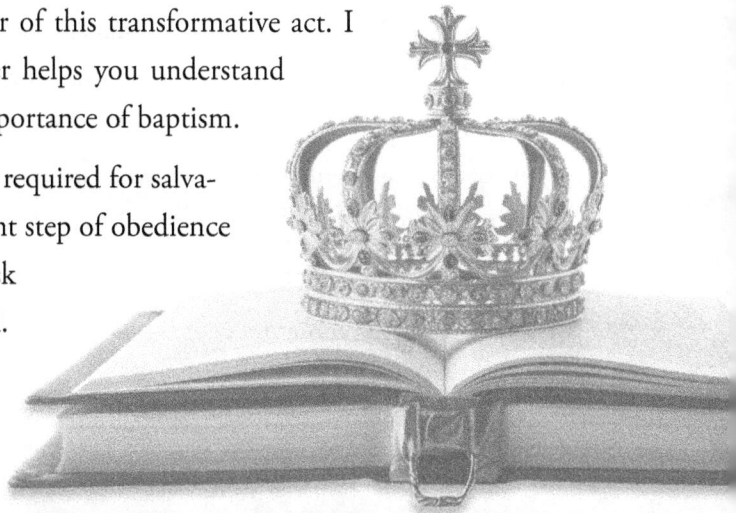

> And when they had come to the place called Calvary, there they crucified Him, and the criminals, one on the right hand and the other on the left...Then one of the criminals who were hanged blasphemed Him, saying, "If You are the Christ, save Yourself and us. But the other, answering, rebuked him, saying, "Do you not even fear God, seeing you are under the same condemnation? And we indeed justly, for we receive the due reward of our deeds; but this Man has done nothing wrong." Then he said to Jesus, "Lord, remember me when You come into Your Kingdom. And Jesus said to him, "Assuredly, I say to you, today you will be with Me in Paradise."
>
> (Luke 23:33, 39-43 NKJV)

How glorious is this encounter? Here is an example of a convicted criminal who accepted his fate for his wrongdoing. He is now on a cross next to Jesus Christ, yet he can recognize Christ's innocence. The criminal recognized Christ's justness, holiness, purity and saving power. He recognized Christ as the Messiah.

Notice how one criminal observed the other criminal mocking Christ and rebuked him. He told him you're in the same situation here on the cross, where's your fear of God. The one criminal still has a heart conducive to conversion. I want you to notice that it was the criminal's heart perception that changed his destiny. In an instance on a cross, his life changed forever. He stepped into his divine destiny by what he believed. His understanding of Christ as Lord caused him to simply ask to be remembered.

You and I have so much to be grateful for because we know that as believers in Christ Jesus, He remembers us when we surrender our hearts before

Him! Surrender. Surrender. Surrender! What a powerful word! When you surrender your heart to the Lord, you too will begin this journey in the Kingdom of God and step into your divine destiny, which has been reserved for you.

I still remember the day I surrendered my heart to the Lord. It was the best choice I have made, and I shall never forget what the Lord has done!

But I want you to understand that this is a biblical example of entering Paradise without water baptism. Jesus told the convicted criminal that he would spend eternity with Him in Paradise.

So, what is this transformative experience called water baptism? In the Christian church water baptism is the religious rite of sprinkling water onto a person's forehead or of immersion in water, symbolizing purification or regeneration and admission to the Christian church.

If we take it a step further, water baptism is a transformative experience that cleanses our souls and immerses us in water. As we examine its meaning, we begin to understand the immense power of this sacred act. Let us seek guidance from the Word of God and uncover the mysteries of baptism together. Let's begin our journey of discovery with an open heart and mind.

WATER BAPTISM SYMBOLIZES A TRANSFORMATIVE REBIRTH.

Water baptism symbolizes a transformative rebirth, marking the beginning of a spiritual journey filled with hope and the potential for positive change. Because of its power and significance, baptism changes our minds and attitudes. To make it plain, symbolically, you are completely submerged in the water. This is now your new birth.

The Doctrine of Baptisms

The doctrine of baptisms teaches the believer that Scripture mentions more than water baptism.

> Of the doctrine of baptisms, of laying on of hands, of resurrection of the dead, and of eternal judgment.
>
> (Hebrews 6:2 NKJV)

In other words, there is baptism by water, baptism into Christ's death, baptism in the Holy Spirit, baptism of repentance, and baptism with fire. These are all different types of baptisms illustrated in Scripture. Being that water baptism is our focus of discussion, I am reminded of my younger days in the church. I recall my own experiences of being water-baptized. But even before I was baptized, I was christened. I was dedicated to the Lord by my mother and father as an infant.

I remember being baptized at Trinity Church of God in Christ. My Pastor, Sam Watkins Sr., a great man of God, was also my uncle. As a young man, I understood what I was doing. I was a believer in Christ Jesus and knew Him as my Lord and Savior.

I, like many of you, grew up in church. As I became a young adult, I moved from the local area where I was raised in Fresno, California. I moved to sunny Southern California. I remember simply desiring a new start in life. I loved the country-style living in Fresno. My father had built a house in a good part of Fresno, the far Westside. I had a good upbringing; I was gifted to play an instrument (the drums), and my sister, Leah Meux, was and has always been a dynamic singer. I know she received that gift from my mother, who passed it down because my mother could and can still sing.

The Breaking Point

My uncle, Sam, would take me fishing and hunting with my cousins. My family loved these hobbies. I enjoyed them, but I wanted to move to the big city. My parents separated and I went through a season of wandering and personal uncertainty. At this point, I really knew I was ready to get out of Fresno. Through the course of time, moving, relocating, and finding employment in another city, I strayed away from the gospel. I stopped going to church. I stopped listening to the Word of God. I found myself like the prodigal son in a big world, making poor choices.

Over the years, I always knew I had a call on my life. I've always been someone who never could get away with anything. My destiny has always been to live for God. But I then spent many years truly just hurt and disappointed, which made me careless.

I realized over the years that the Lord would simply keep me and preserve me when I wasn't doing a great job of caring for myself in reckless and riotous living. The one thing I could do right in this time span was work. So, through my season of "lack of identity," I spent a lot of time on the job. I became what you'd call a workaholic. I engulfed myself in accumulating material possessions, working long hours, and attempting to use things to make me happy. But the truth was, nothing was filling the void in my heart.

One day, I was home alone, my wife and family away for the day, and I found myself watching a sermon by T.D. Jakes. I don't recall the title of the sermon, but I found myself prostrate before the Lord in tears. At that moment, I realized that I needed to rededicate myself to the Lord.

I had unknowingly reached my first breaking point in adult life, a moment of the greatest strain and stress I had ever experienced. Things around me were out of order, and several broken relationships were now weighing heavily on me.

Now, here's the point. At a low point in my life, the deliverer, whose name is Jesus Christ, visited my heart. We had a very intense conversation, which began with the release of my hardened heart. What makes this even more touching for me is that I wasn't at a church service. There wasn't a preacher telling me everything I did was wrong. There wasn't a minister telling me I'm going to hell. This experience with God simply showed me that the Lord was willing. The Lord was willing to meet me where I was. What a gracious Father! He'll meet you at your lowest point and turn your entire life around.

I immediately got up from my bedroom floor and, within 24 hours, joined a local church. I dedicated myself to serving God, and after some time, I was baptized in water. But this time, when I was baptized, I was much more aware of who I was in Christ and much more grateful for how the Lord kept me and brought me back into the Kingdom of God.

Water baptism is an outer expression of your salvation by acknowledging the ways of God. John the Baptist baptized Jesus according to Scripture.

> When He had been baptized, Jesus came up immediately from the water; and behold, the heavens were opened to Him, and He saw the Spirit of God descending like a dove and alighting upon Him. (Matthew 3:16 NKJV)

What is very interesting about the context of Scripture here is that in Matthew 3:15, Jesus called His baptism by John the Baptist the fulfillment of all righteousness. I submit to you that this is a description of divine order. So, you can rest assured that by following the Lord in believer's baptism, we are obeying Christ and showing Him that we are extremely grateful for what He has accomplished for us.

A Public Declaration

Through water baptism, we experience the blessing of committing ourselves to Christ through our public display. It symbolizes our spiritual death, being buried with Christ, and then our resurrection to new life in Him. Baptism is a powerful representation of our old self dying and being raised up as a new creation in Christ. Through baptism, we proclaim to the world that we have been transformed by the power of God and are now living for Him. We also commit ourselves to following Jesus and His teachings, knowing that He has washed away our sins through His death on the cross.

Baptism reminds us to die to self and live for Christ every day. Just as we were submerged in the water during our baptism, we are called to be fully immersed in our relationship with Christ and allow Him to guide every aspect of our lives. Baptism is an ongoing symbol of surrendering to God and allowing His will to be done in us.

Baptism also serves as a unifying act for believers. When we are baptized, we become part of the body of Christ and join in fellowship with other believers who have been washed clean by the blood of Jesus. This unity among Christians

BAPTISM REMINDS US TO DIE TO SELF AND LIVE FOR CHRIST EVERY DAY.

strengthens and encourages us in our faith journey, knowing that we are not alone but part of a larger family united through our belief in Jesus.

It is a public declaration of our faith in Jesus and our commitment to following Him. It is not just a symbolic act, but it holds great significance as we publicly acknowledge that we have been saved by grace through faith in Christ. This declaration can inspire others who may be considering following Jesus and remind us to stay true to our faith and continue growing in our relationship with Him.

Jesus' declaration, "Go into all the world and make disciples, baptizing them," was a clear directive to the church to embrace the practice of baptism. This, indeed, is the great commission for believers. This is what I truly believe, according to the Word. Likewise, the Holy Spirit's exhortation in Acts 2:38, "Repent and be baptized," serves as a personal appeal to each believer to experience baptism. I want you to see something very powerful that comes out of this context of Scripture.

In Acts 2:37, the Scripture tells us that Apostle Peter, while ministering this gospel to the house of Israel, said, "that God has made this Jesus, whom you crucified, both Lord and Christ," and the Bible says when he said this, "they were cut to the heart." I call this a breaking point. This point in Apostle Peter's message in the Holy Spirit opened an opportunity for the house of Israel to leave the place of knowingly crucifying the Savior to a place of renewed mind through repentance and baptism. The Scripture teaches that they'd receive the remission of sins and receive the Holy Spirit.

The Bride of Christ

One who refuses to be baptized could be like a wife who refuses to accept her wedding ring after saying "Yes" to marriage. As the body of Christ, we are the bride of Christ.

> Let us be glad and rejoice and give Him glory, for the marriage of the Lamb has come, and His wife has made herself

Baptism: Take the First Step

ready. And to her it was granted to be arrayed in fine linen, clean and bright, for the fine linen is the righteous acts of the saints. Then he said to me, "Write: 'Blessed are those who are called to the marriage supper of the Lamb!'" And he said to me, "These are the true sayings of God."

(Revelation 19:7-9 NKJV)

In other words, how can our relationship with Christ be in right-standing if we refuse to follow Him and if we are ashamed of Him before others? I submit to you that baptism is one of those "righteous acts of the saints" described here in the text.

Guilt and Shame

Ashamed is a very interesting word. It refers to being afraid and feeling shame, which can prevent one from doing something or cause a reluctance to say or do something because of fear of others. The *1828 Webster's Dictionary* adds that ashamed is to be confused by a consciousness of guilt or of inferiority; by the mortification of pride; by failure or disappointment; a painful sensation excited by a consciousness of guilt, or of having done something which injures reputation; or by that which nature or modesty prompts us to conceal. Shame is particularly excited by the disclosure of actions which, in the view of men, are mean and degrading. Hence, it is often or always manifested by a downcast look or by blushes, called confusion of the face. Apostle Paul tells us something very profound.

> For I am not ashamed of the gospel of Christ, for it is the power of God to salvation for everyone who believes, for the Jew first and also for the Greek. For in it the righteousness

of God is revealed from faith to faith; as it is written, "The just shall live by faith. (Romans 1:16-17 NKJV)

So, one of the ways that we remove or dismantle the influences of shame is by faith and not our own faith, but faith in the finished work of Jesus. According to the revelation of Scripture, your faith can be seen through your actions. One of these ways is through the expression of water baptism.

Baptism is not something to fear or step away from because of shame but something that causes your light to appear! Just ask Christ. In the book of Hebrews 12:2, the writer declares that Jesus "for the joy that was set before him endured the cross, despising the shame." In other words, even though this was not in relation to baptism, it's a description of the victory given to you by the blood of Jesus to overcome shame. Jesus Christ disregarded it, ignored it, and even took the disgrace of the cross on our behalf that we triumph in Him.

Water baptism represents Jesus's death, burial, and resurrection, showing that you have died to your old self and been raised to new life in Christ. This act of obedience not only demonstrates your faith but also serves as a powerful witness to others. It declares that you are no longer ashamed of the gospel but rather proud to be identified with it.

In addition to water baptism, we should also not be ashamed to share our testimony with others. Our story of how God has transformed our lives through His grace and love can inspire others and bring glory to God. By boldly sharing our testimony, we are not only breaking the chains of shame in our own lives but also helping others find freedom in Christ.

As believers, we should also not be ashamed to live out our faith in everyday life. This means standing up for what is right and living according to God's Word, even when it may go against popular opinion or social norms. We shouldn't be afraid to speak the truth in love and let our actions reflect the love of Christ.

Being unashamed of the gospel means having an unwavering faith in Christ and boldly living out that faith through our words, actions, and beliefs. It means not being afraid to stand up for what we believe in and proudly declaring our identity as children of God. Let us strive to live a life unashamed of the gospel, shining our light brightly for all to see and leading others to the hope and salvation found in Jesus Christ. So go ahead, take that step of faith, and publicly declare your love for Christ through water baptism. Share your testimony with those around you, and let your light shine without shame! Score points for the Kingdom of Heaven by courageously living out your faith each day.

Baptism identifies us publicly with Christ and His church—specifically, the remnant church that maintains biblical truth in every generation. In Chapter 7, we'll discover our place in this faithful company of believers.

Prayer for the Gift of Baptism

Lord, thank You for the precious gift of baptism so that I can publicly declare my love and passion for You. Lord, I ask for Your goodness and blessings to be poured out on me, your faithful servant. I pray that You would work deeply within my heart and soul to renew and refresh me each day. I ask this in faith, in Jesus' name. Amen.

CHAPTER SEVEN

THE REMNANT CHURCH

What is a remnant? Throughout history, God has always preserved a faithful remnant—those who remain true to His Word and purposes despite cultural pressures to compromise. This chapter explores what it means to be part of God's remnant in our generation. We'll examine the characteristics, calling, and responsibilities of those who choose to stand firm in their faith while extending God's love to a world in need.

The word remnant, according to the *Oxford Dictionary*, means a small remaining quantity of something, a remainder or a residue. The Hebrew word for remnant is *sheerith,* which means survivors, residual, or those who have escaped. If you are reading this book, I believe you are a part of the Lord's remnant, a part of the body of Christ, a part of the end-time harvest. You're the church or those who have escaped the temptations of the world and are separated as unto the Lord. You've been anointed with the Holy Spirit and redeemed by the blood of

Christ. As part of the Lord's remnant, you possess the strength and resilience to overcome any challenge. I encourage you to embrace your identity as a member of the body of Christ and let your light shine brightly in the world, inspiring positive change by the Word of God.

Apostle Peter says this:

> By which have been given to us exceedingly great and precious promises, that through these you may be partakers of the divine nature, having escaped the corruption that is in the world through lust. (2 Peter 1:4 NKJV)

What does this mean? It means that because you are in Christ and have been given eternal life by faith in the finished work of Jesus. We have avoided a future separated from God, and better yet, we are receivers of the Father's presence and all His goodness.

The remnant church is those who have escaped the desires of dishonesty, greed, and deception that come into the world through lust. The remnant church is those who refuse to be persuaded by erroneous teachings and doctrines. I want you to shout out, "I refuse!" I want you to recognize that you're a blood-bought believer. You've been bought with a price.

Scripture teaches us that we are to glorify God in body and spirit. We understand that the remnant may mean something different to each of us. We all come from different walks of life and beliefs. But, most importantly, we understand that the truth is the Word of God. The Word of God is the standard. The Word teaches that when the enemy comes in, like a flood, the Spirit of the Lord will lift a standard. That standard is the Word of God. This is the truth to which you and I have been called.

With today's technology, social media outlets, the internet, YouTube, and other platforms, deception is at an all-time high. People want money, possessions, and fame, and often, their desire for these things holds a higher value in their hearts than biblical morality and truth. I believe this is why the remnant church is called to take a stand regarding the Word of God in love, truth, and righteousness.

One of the ways we're able to express these keys is in the Lord's righteousness. Righteousness is defined as being in right standing with God or the approval of God. You've been called to stand in the Lord's righteousness based on what Christ has accomplished. Apostle Paul said that "you are the righteousness of God in Him" (2 Cor. 5:21). I believe that in this generation, we are set to see a mighty turnaround, a mighty harvest, the mighty hand of God materialized, in our families, our communities, our relationships, and the systems of this age because we serve the righteous King. Rest assured, it's going to happen through the glory of God revealed in us. The Word of the Lord declares:

> For the earnest expectation of the creature waiteth for the manifestation of the sons of God. (Romans 8:19)

As believers, we are called to manifest God's glory in everything we do. His strength, power, and anointing permeate and penetrate atmospheres, entering boardroom meetings and hospital rooms and going where we may not be able to physically go. How does this occur, you may ask? It occurs through the Spirit of God and His Word. It occurs as we stand in faith, living according to biblical principles, even when it goes against the current culture and trends.

The Fourth Man in the Fire

Remember the three Hebrew boys, Shadrach, Meshach, and Abednego, when they were cast into the fiery furnace in Daniel Chapter 3. They were cast into the fiery furnace for refusing to bow to the statue created by King Nebuchadnezzar. I encourage you to read it; it's a good read.

The three Hebrew boys were associated with other administrators, governors, and counselors who accused them of not bowing to King Nebuchadnezzar's statue. The king issued a decree that when the music was played, everyone had to bow to his statue; if not, you'd be put to death. The king confronted them, and it was determined that the three Hebrew boys were to be thrown into the fiery furnace because they would not bow. As a matter of fact, the king requested that it be turned up seven times hotter because of their defiance of his decree. I'll tell you that God delivered them. They were thrown into the fiery furnace, but in that place, Scripture says:

GOD KNOWS HOW TO GET THE ATTENTION OF YOUR ADVERSARY.

> "Look!" he answered, "I see four men loose, walking in the midst of the fire; and they are not hurt, and the form of the fourth is like the Son of God." (Daniel 3:25 NKJV)

God knows how to get the attention of your adversary. They'll have to recognize that the presence of God (the glory) is on you. I'm sure you'll agree that our God is mighty. The God you serve is the great deliverer. God brought them out of that situation without the fire having any power over them; their hair wasn't singed, nor were their garments, and they didn't smell like smoke. Now, that's the kind of God we serve.

I want you to be encouraged because He is no respecter of persons. If He did it for the three Hebrew boys, He will do it for you. The Scriptures say, "Jesus Christ the same yesterday, today and forever." Here's even better news: that same miracle-working God is within you. The Bible says, "Greater is He that is in you than he that is in the world" (1 John 4:4). God has given the power and authority through Christ to you to overcome any deception or temptation that comes your way. You're the remnant church, the called of God, those separated to be partakers of His glory.

The remnant church stays rooted in truth. We are those who align ourselves with the Word of God and seek His guidance in all things. But be reminded that the power of God in you is not just for your own benefit but also for the sake of others. When we stand in righteousness and live according to God's standards, we become a light to those around us, even to those in positions of authority like King Nebuchadnezzar. Our actions and words have a powerful impact on those who are lost or searching for the truth.

I want you to notice what Apostle Paul told his spiritual son, Timothy, regarding a time to come.

> For the time will come when they will not endure sound doctrine, but according to their own desires, because they have itching ears, they will heap up for themselves teachers; and they will turn their ears away from the truth and be turned aside to fables. (2 Timothy 4:3-4 NKJV)

God is calling us to a generation that is more interested in their own desires than the truth of God's Word. But you and I are Kingdom citizens (Phil. 3:20). We represent those who won't be turned aside to fables, tricked, or

WELCOME TO THE KINGDOM

led away by deception. I want you to pay special attention to this term turned aside. It is a medical term that describes a dislocated bone. Apostle Paul uses this analogy to describe one who has strayed from the teachings of truth, the same as if a bone has been dislocated. Those who have been turned aside will be those who are following fiction, fabrications, or stories that are not based upon the truth of God's Word.

Thank you, Lord, for grace. Mighty are You, Lord. Right here, I want you to thank the Lord for the eyes of our understanding being enlightened that He would allow us to know the hope of His calling and the riches of His inheritance in us (Ephesians 1:8). This is a good place to thank the Lord for His grace because He saw fit to call us out of darkness into His marvelous light. This is a good place to thank the Lord for His mercy, grace, and favor. Hallelujah.

I believe that as Kingdom citizens, God has divinely called us to be carriers of Christ's nature, character, and authority. God is a miracle worker, and He desires to work miracles in your life. You're to know Him by His attributes and His ability to perform miracles, signs, and wonders. But get this, He not only desires this in your situation, but He also desires it in the lives of those connected to you.

I'm once again reminded of Scripture. Let us look closely at the Book of Acts.

> To whom He also presented Himself alive after His suffering by many infallible proofs. (Acts 1:3 NKJV)

Don't miss this: Christ's resurrection presented the Apostles with "many infallible proofs." The word infallible comes from the Greek word *tekmerion,* which means sure signs, indisputable evidence, or what is unmistakable or known.

I recall when New Covenant Ministry was founded. Lady Desiree and I began holding small gatherings at our home, reading Scripture and in prayer. Initially, that was all we intended to do. Before long, we were holding these same gatherings in our backyard to provide space. We had some friends who were anointed in singing and playing instruments. They started coming to our home, and in an instant, we were worshipping the Lord. The next thing I know, we've got a band, weekly at our home, and we're speaking the Word of God and in prayer. Within a few weeks, we decided to call a real estate friend of ours and inquire about a rental space to hold services. She knew the perfect person. We met the owner of a complex, and we had an agreement in place the same day. Look at God!

For Such a Time as This

I believe the remnant church will be recognizable by the open display of God's inherent power working in the life of the believer in the Holy Spirit. You and I have been called for such a time as this. We've been called to reveal the presence of God. We've been called to see the types of manifestation that only God can perform. In our own ministry, we've seen the blind see and the deaf begin to hear. It's a time of the miraculous. It's a time of infallible proofs.

WE'VE BEEN CALLED TO REVEAL THE PRESENCE OF GOD.

One of the ways that this revelation becomes a reality in your life is by getting connected to a Bible-based church filled with the Spirit of God. Don't get me wrong, I know we're living in a time of struggles, mishaps, confusion, and more. We're living in a time of wars, nation against nation, famines, pestilences, home evictions, financial strain, political dysfunction, and unrelenting family turmoil.

But let me remind you that Jesus said in His Word that all these types of things would come about in the last days, but you and I are not to be troubled. You and I are to stand fast on the Word of God in prayer and supplication. You and I have the mandate of thanking God for the abundance of all things, no matter the trial or tribulation. Apostle James said that we are to "count it all joy when faced with divers' temptations" meaning this is the time we release our faith in the finished work of Jesus. This is the time you and I declare victory over sickness, disease, and any misfortune.

The Psalmist declared:

> Many are the afflictions of the righteous, But the Lord
> delivers him out of them all. (Psalm 34:19 NKJV)

Please don't ignore the "out of them all" portion of the text. You're the remnant; something good must happen for you because the Spirit of God dwells within you. You're like King David; you're called never to lose a battle because you're on the Lord's side and you have the Father's heart. The key is to hold fast to the Word of God.

The Lord has revealed to me the importance of the remnant church. Just as there was a remnant in the time of Elijah, God has a remnant church today. This is a group of believers who unashamedly live out their faith and stand firm in the face of trials and persecution.

The remnant church is small in number compared to the rest of the world, we are strong in faith and unwavering in our commitment to follow Christ. We are not swayed by the ways of the world or tempted to compromise for acceptance or comfort. Instead, we hold onto God's promises and trust in His deliverance from all afflictions.

Do you know why you can give God praise? Because you have His Word on the matter. Do you know why you should shout for victory? Because you have God's Word on the situation. This is how you know the grace of God is working on your behalf. It's literally because you won't stop speaking God's Word.

Our Voice Will Be Heard

Here's the last point I want to make regarding the remnant. Revelation 2:19-29 speaks about a church called Thyatira that was corrupted by the spirit of Jezebel. What you find in this text is there are two types of churches within one church. There are those who follow the doctrine of Jezebel. The teachings of Jezebel are teachings to manipulate, deceive, seduce, and persuade using witchcraft and to do whatever she can to silence the prophetic voice.

There was also a body of believers, in this text, that would keep the Word of God, who the Scriptures say would rule or have power over the nations and shine as the morning star. When the Scriptures refer to ruling or having power over the nations, it means that the voice of the remnant church would be heard and have influence on the earth. I submit to you that this is the time for the remnant church to declare the wonderful works of God. To speak the truth of God's Word and see results. The morning star referenced in Scripture meant that you and I will reflect Christ and function in His authority. We're to see sick bodies healed, families delivered, loved ones coming off the streets, and industries turned over to the spiritual authority of Christ.

I declare to you that this is a time for the prophetic voice of the sons and daughters of God to be heard. It is a time for the true church to rise and take authority over the powers of darkness, just as the Scriptures say:

> For we do not wrestle against flesh and blood, but against principalities, against powers, against the rulers of the darkness of this age, against spiritual hosts of wickedness in the heavenly places. (Ephesians 6:12)

As believers, we have been given the authority to speak and decree truth during deception. We have been given power over the works of the enemy with the truth of God's Word.

The remnant of the true church, the body of Christ, is a beacon of hope in a world filled with despair. Chosen from among the millions who have lived and died, they are few in number but mighty in faith, spreading love and redemption to all who seek it. The remnant is a group of special individuals who have made a commitment to Jesus. They are determined to serve Him with all their might and love, no matter what obstacles they may encounter. Their focus and will are unwavering, and they will continue to serve Christ with all their heart and soul.

In the remnant church, we find comfort and strength in the unwavering authority of the Bible. Our faith is built upon the bedrock of God's Word, which guides us toward a life of righteousness and purity and empowers us to stand tall in the face of adversity. The remnant church signifies a resilient fellowship of believers who steadfastly cling to God's commandments and teachings, even in the face of widespread apostasy or societal moral decay, serving as beacons of hope and inspiration for all.

The remnant church stands firmly on the foundation of God's Word. Chapter 8 will explore how the Bible guides and grounds us in Kingdom living.

Prayer for the Remnant Church

Your Word tells us that You have always had a remnant, those who refused to bow their knees to false gods. Oh Lord, watch over us, protect us from evil, and guide our path as we faithfully serve and follow You. May the name of Jesus be lifted up and glorified in every corner of the globe. We decree it by faith, in Jesus' name. Amen.

CHAPTER EIGHT

THE BIBLE

G od's Word stands as our unshakeable foundation, our guide for life, and our source of truth in an ever-changing world. This chapter explores how to approach, understand, and apply Scripture in ways that transform our daily lives. More than just an ancient text, the Bible remains living and active, capable of speaking into every situation we face. We'll discover practical ways to engage with Scripture that deepen our relationship with God and strengthen our faith.

The Holy Scripture is divided into the Old and New Testaments. The books of Malachi and Matthew mark the end of a 400-year era known as the divinely ordained silence. Although no new Scriptures were written during this period, our faith sustained us, and God's presence remained palpable.

During the four hundred years of silence, significant events occurred in Israel and the surrounding nations. The Jews suffered under different foreign rulers, such as the Persians, Greeks, and Romans. These rulers brought with them

their cultures, religions, and customs, which influenced the Jewish people. Important Jewish religious sects, such as the Pharisees and Sadducees, emerged during this time. These sects had different beliefs and practices, which shaped the religious landscape of Israel at that time.

Additionally, many historical events occurred during these four hundred years that would impact the world for centuries to come. These include the rise and fall of powerful empires, such as the Greeks and Romans, which would impact the spread of Christianity in the future.

Despite the lack of written Scriptures during this time, God was still at work in the lives of His people. He raised prophets like John the Baptist to prepare the way for Jesus' ministry. He also orchestrated events that would lead to Jesus' birth in Bethlehem, fulfilling prophecies from centuries before.

The four hundred years of silence may have been a time without any new written Scriptures, but it was not a time without God's presence or influence. It could be said that this period served as a bridge between the Old and New Testaments, preparing the world for the coming of Jesus Christ and the establishment of Christianity. It serves as a reminder that even in times when we may feel like God is silent, He is still at work, and His plans are unfolding. It also highlights the importance of seeing how God is working in our lives and the world around us. So, while this period may be known as the "400 years of silence," it was far from being a time without significance or meaning in God's grand plan for humanity.

The Arrival of the Kingdom

Other writings, such as the Apocrypha, do not form part of the accepted canon of Scripture. These writings are documented as lacking authenticity, doubtful authorship, and uninspired writing. As a result, the only books of the Bible are the Old and New Testaments. Even though the Bible is made up of sixty-six books, or what we call the canon of Scripture, it has one message: the establishment of the Kingdom of God through Christ Jesus. Scripture teaches:

> And saying, "The time is fulfilled, and the Kingdom of God is at hand. Repent, and believe in the gospel."
>
> (Mark 1:15 NKJV)

This verse highlights the core message of the Bible, which is the arrival of God's Kingdom through Jesus and the call for repentance and belief in the gospel. The Old Testament lays the foundation for the Kingdom, with prophecies and promises of a coming Messiah who will save God's people. The New Testament reveals this promised Messiah as Jesus Christ, who came to fulfill God's plan of redemption for all humanity.

Through Christ's death and resurrection, we are reconciled with God and given eternal life in His Kingdom. As believers, we need to understand the significance of both sections of the Bible. The Old Testament shows us the need for a Savior and prepares us for the coming of Jesus Christ, while the New Testament shows us how that promise was fulfilled and how, by the power of the Holy Spirit, we can live in His Kingdom here on Earth. Apostle Paul writes to the church of Galatia:

THE OLD TESTAMENT LAYS THE FOUNDATION FOR THE KINGDOM.

> Therefore the law was our tutor to bring us to Christ, that we might be justified by faith. But after faith has come, we are no longer under a tutor. (Galatians 3:24-25 NKJV)

WELCOME TO THE KINGDOM

This Scripture reveals the purpose of the Old Testament, which is to lead us to Christ and prepare us for Christ's coming. The way we accomplish our preparation for His coming is by faith. The Bible is not just a collection of stories or teachings but a cohesive message of God's love and plan for humanity. We need to study and understand both the Old and New Testaments to fully grasp this message of faith in the finished work of Jesus and how it applies to our lives today. One Scriptural example of this comes from Apostle Paul's message to the church of Corinth:

> Now all these things happened unto them for ensamples,
> and they are written for our admonition, upon whom the
> ends of the world are come.
> (1 Corinthians 10:11, Authorized KJV)

The Old Testament provides examples and helps us understand the New Testament. Many of the teachings and concepts in the New Testament have roots in the Old Testament. So, as new covenant believers, we understand that these ensamples were for our admonition and instruction. The term ensamples in the Authorized King James Version has significant meaning. Ensamples is the Greek word *tupos*, which means pattern, copy, or type. Ensamples mean a reliable precedent for others to then follow or a model for imitation. This means that the stories and events recorded in the Old Testament are not just for historical purposes but also serve as examples for us to learn from. We can see how God dealt with His people in the past, both in their successes and failures, and apply those lessons to our own lives. The Bible is a living book with timeless truths that can be applied to any situation or circumstance we may face.

HE HAS AN AMAZING FUTURE PRESCRIBED FOR YOU.

As we continue to read and learn from the Word of God, may we always remember its ultimate purpose, which is to reveal God's Kingdom through Jesus and bring salvation to all who believe. Let us also be reminded that as believers, we are called according to the Father's plan and purpose for our lives. It has been through the Holy Scriptures that I have found my purpose in life.

It's truly a blessing from God that as you spend time with Him, He's able to show you that you're His own. In His purpose, you will find the specific fulfillment that you desire in life. The Word of God is not only a place of refuge as the Proverbs says, "the name of the Lord is a strong tower and the righteous run into it and are safe," but it's also a place of peace, prosperity, destiny, hope, and loving-kindness. The purpose of God is sure. The Father intends to produce His plan for your life before your very eyes. He has an amazing future prescribed for you.

The Prophet Jeremiah said it this way:

> For I know the thoughts that I think toward you, says the Lord, thoughts of peace and not of evil, to give you a future and a hope. (Jeremiah 29:11 NKJV)

God's Living Word

Please be assured that the Bible is not just a historical record or a book of rules to follow, it's not a novel written by your favorite author, but it is God's living Word. Its writings are inspired by the Holy Spirit. There have been many men who have contributed to the articulation of Scripture, but there has only been one author, one penman, which is the Holy Spirit. The Word of God speaks to us today just as it did to people thousands of years ago. As we study and meditate on its message, we are transformed by the power of God's Spirit working in us.

Furthermore, the Bible provides guidance and wisdom for daily life. It teaches us about love, forgiveness, mercy, faith, patience, grace, and more. It shows us how to navigate the challenges and trials of life and how to have a close relationship with God the Father through the Son, Jesus Christ, who is now in the person of the Holy Spirit.

WE ARE CALLED TO LIVE OUT THE PRINCIPLES OF THE KINGDOM OF GOD ON EARTH.

By the same token, the Bible reveals God's character and His desire for us to have intimacy and fellowship with Him. By reading about Jesus's life and teachings in New Testament Scripture, we can better understand who God is and how He wants us to live.

The Bible is a guide to Kingdom living, and as the Apostle Luke said, I want us to focus on this subject a bit.

> Do not fear, little flock, for it is your Father's good pleasure to give you the Kingdom. (Luke 12:32 NKJV)

Kingdom refers to the way God does things, including His rulership, reign, royalty, and dominion. It is a way of life that encompasses every aspect of our being—physical, emotional, and spiritual. Scripture teaches that we are spirit, soul, and body. As believers, we are called to live out the principles of the Kingdom of God on Earth.

Kingdom Living

The Bible contains many teachings and parables about the Kingdom of God. These teachings emphasize the importance of understanding and applying these principles in our daily lives. Jesus taught extensively about the Kingdom and demonstrated it through His actions and miracles.

One key aspect of Kingdom living is living in obedience to God's will. To fully experience the blessings and abundance promised in the Kingdom, we must submit ourselves to God's authority and follow His commandments. This includes loving one another, serving others, and being good stewards of the resources God has given us.

Another important aspect of Kingdom living is having a mindset of abundance rather than scarcity. In the Kingdom, we are called to have faith that God will provide for our needs and trust in His timing and plan for our lives. This requires us to let go of fear, worry, and selfishness and instead focus on living with gratitude and generosity towards others.

In addition to personal transformation, Kingdom living also involves working towards bringing about positive change in our communities and society. As ambassadors of the Kingdom, we are called to be agents of love, justice, and peace wherever we go. Apostle Paul said:

> Now then, we are *ambassadors for Christ*, as though God were pleading through us: we implore *you* on Christ's behalf, be reconciled to God. (2 Corinthians 5:20 NKJV)

Reconciliation=Peace

Overall, embracing Kingdom living means surrendering our desires and ambitions to God's will, trusting in His goodness and sovereignty, and actively living out the principles of love, service, and justice in our daily lives. This principle becomes a reality as we keep before us the God who reconciled us to Himself through Christ Jesus and has given us His word of reconciliation and ministry of reconciliation. You may ask, what is reconciliation?

Reconciliation is the Greek word *katallage,* which means restoration as the result of Christ precisely exchanging His righteousness (blood) for our guilt. Reconciliation is a restoration of the favor of God to sinners who repent and put their trust in the expiatory death of Christ. Reconciliation is the coming to oneness with the Father and the Son. Reconciliation is a fundamental concept in biblical understanding that emphasizes the restoration of a broken relationship between God and humanity. It symbolizes the process of making peace with God through Jesus Christ, who offered Himself as a sacrifice to atone for our sins.

May we continually seek to grow in our understanding and application of the Kingdom of God on Earth. Let us strive each day to live as citizens of the Kingdom, bringing hope and light to a world that desperately needs it. Let us be vessels of God's love and grace, shining brightly for all to see. I submit that we will never forget that our true home is not here on Earth but in the eternal Kingdom where we will one day reside with our King forevermore.

I believe that we should allow this knowledge to reshape us in our actions as we seek to build the Kingdom of God. I pray that the Father will grant us the ability to continue to keep our focus on the goal, which is to bring Him glory and spread His love to all. And may we never lose sight of the fact that we are privileged and privileged indeed to be a part of such a glorious Kingdom. Let's embrace every opportunity to spread its light and beauty wherever we go, knowing that with our outward expressions of our love for God, we are building an eternal inheritance in the Kingdom of God. Strive for excellence in all areas of your lives as you establish the Kingdom of God here on Earth.

As It Is in Heaven

I would like to shed a little light on establishing the Kingdom of God on Earth. The Scripture teaches us that God seeks to establish His Kingdom in the lives of His children, which you are. As you seek God's Word, you'll find that Jesus tells us in His Word,

> Nor will they say, 'See here!' or 'See there!' For indeed, the Kingdom of God is within you. (Luke 17:21 NKJV)

This may seem like a paradox, as we often think of the Kingdom of God as a physical place we will go to after death. However, Jesus is reminding us that the Kingdom of God starts within our hearts and lives now as we surrender to His reign and allow Him to transform us from the inside out.

As citizens of this Kingdom, we are called to live differently than the world around us. We are called to be salt and light in a dark world, bringing hope and love wherever we go. This can look different for each person, but it means living a life that reflects the values and teachings of our King.

Kingdom living is a reality from God's Word. Our Bible contains everything we need to know about our past, our present, and our future. The Hebrew writer said it like this, "Jesus is the same yesterday, today and forever." The truth of who we are is in His Word. Matthew, the Apostle, a messenger of the teachings of Christ, said this:

It is written, 'Man shall not live by bread alone, but by every word that proceeds from the mouth of God.'

(Matthew 4:4 NKJV)

As believers, we should take this verse to heart and understand the importance of nourishing our souls with the Word of God, just as we nourish our bodies with food. Reading and meditating on the Bible helps us gain a deeper understanding of God's will for our lives and how to live according to His principles. It also helps us strengthen our faith and draw closer to God as Kingdom citizens. The Word of God is our strong tower, a place of safety and protection.

The Bible is a source of comfort and guidance even during difficult times. In times of trials and tribulations, we can always turn to the Word of God for encouragement and strength. It reminds us that God is always with us and will never forsake us. This is a good place to reflect on how good God is. I'm sure we can all look back over our lives and see how God never left us or forsook us.

GOD IS ALWAYS WITH US AND WILL NEVER FORSAKE US.

When I was growing up, the saints in the church would say, "When I look back over my life." This statement was an indication that God somehow, in some way, kept them through every situation. The Bible gives us a clear picture of God's redemptive power always at work in our lives. The book of Psalms is filled with verses that offer solace and hope during tough times:

Your word is a lamp to my feet and a light to my path.

(Psalm 119:105 NKJV)

As we read and study the Bible, we can gain wisdom and understanding from God's perspective. This enables us to make wise decisions and stay on the right path. It also helps us discern truth from falsehood and recognize the enemy's deceitful tactics. The Bible is truly a powerful tool for spiritual growth and development.

Practice Makes Perfect

In addition to reading and meditating on the Word of God, we should also put it into practice. Some may question why we must practice. But practice is the actual application or use of the idea, method, theory, or belief. As James 1:22 speaks, "But be doers of the word, and not hearers only, deceiving yourselves." Our faith should be reflected in our actions and how we live our lives. By obeying the teachings of the Bible, we can experience God's blessings and live a life pleasing to Him.

As we read God's Word, speak His Word, and are doers of His Word, these promises are fulfilled in our lives, our faith is then strengthened, and we are reminded that God is faithful. We are also able to see that God's Word is powerful and effective, able to transform our hearts and minds.

This transformation leads to a changed and renewed life, where we can live according to God's will and purpose. Therefore, let us make it a priority to read and study the Bible so that we may grow in our faith and relationship with God. As we do so, we will see the impact. Let us never underestimate the power of the Word of God. As one gospel preacher who I deeply respect says, "The Word of God is the most powerful thing in the Earth, period!"

A Communal Experience

Some concluding thoughts are that the Bible is a source of fellowship and a Kingdom community. There are many examples in the Bible of individuals coming together to support one another, pray together, and grow in their faith. One example is found in Acts 2:42-47 which describes how the early believers devoted themselves to teaching, fellowship, breaking bread, and prayer.

Studying the Bible can be a communal experience. When we gather with other believers to discuss and study Scripture together, we can learn from each other and grow in our understanding of God's Word. I encourage you to connect with a church community that offers mentorship, discipleship, sonship, and leadership to enhance your spiritual growth.

Finally, let us never forget the ultimate purpose of studying the Bible, which is to know God more intimately. The Bible is not just for gaining knowledge, but it is also a means for us to connect with our Creator and develop a deeper relationship with Him. We should always approach the Word of God with reverence, humility, and a desire to encounter Him through each page. While reading Scripture is vital, truly engaging with God's Word requires meditation and memorization. Chapter 9 will teach us how to internalize and apply biblical truth effectively.

Prayer for Wisdom and Understanding

Lord, I pray that You, the God of our Lord Jesus Christ, the Father of glory, will give me the spirit of wisdom and revelation in the knowledge of You according to Your Word, that the eyes of my understanding will be enlightened; that I may know what is the hope of Your calling, what are the glorious riches of Your inheritance in the saints, and what is the exceeding greatness of Your power toward me because I believe, according to the working of Your mighty power, in Jesus' name. Amen!

Chapter Nine

SCRIPTURE MEMORY AND MEDITATION

I n a world inundated with distractions and noise, the practice of Scripture memory and meditation can seem outdated. Yet, these are not just
spiritual disciplines—they are profound encounters with the living Word
of God. They are invitations to step into divine transformation, where the
written Word becomes a living, breathing reality in our lives.

I submit to you that God's Word is more than mere text on a page—it
is alive and powerful. The Scripture declares that "the Word of God is
living and powerful, and sharper than any two-edged sword" (Hebrews
4:12). The word "living" here is the Greek word zao, which means to live,
breathe, and be among the living. This same word is
used to describe our resurrected Lord. Just as Christ
is alive, His Word is filled with divine life and
power. It serves as a supernatural por-
tal into His presence, a bridge between
Heaven and Earth.

When we approach Scrip-
ture, we're not simply
gathering informa-

tion or accumulating biblical knowledge. We are stepping into an encounter with the One who spoke all things into existence. The Word is both the breath of God (2 Timothy 3:16) and a manifestation of Christ Himself, who is called the Living Word (John 1:1, 14). Every time we open the Bible with a hungry heart, we open ourselves to a transformative encounter with the Author, who desires to reveal His heart, His ways, and His purposes to those who seek Him through His Word.

From this perspective, memorizing and meditating on Scripture becomes an act of intimacy, a way to host God's presence in our hearts and minds.

> Your Word I have hidden in my heart, that I might not sin against You. (Psalm 119:11 NKJV)

This declaration from the psalmist reveals a sacred truth: hiding God's Word in our hearts equips us to live victoriously. It's not just about avoiding sin; it's about aligning our thoughts with Heaven's reality. When we memorize Scripture, we carry the mind of Christ into every situation we face.

The Bible is not just a collection of ancient writings; it's a weapon, a tool for transformation. Every verse stored in your heart becomes a reservoir of truth that the Holy Spirit can draw upon to guide, comfort, and empower you. When Jesus was tempted in the wilderness, He didn't argue or negotiate. He quoted Scripture: "It is written…" (Matthew 4:4). That same authority is available to us when we commit His Word to memory.

Practical Methods for Scripture Memory

If memorization feels intimidating, start small and build momentum. Here are some practical methods:

The Layered Approach – Start with single verses and work your way up to longer passages. For example, memorize a verse like Philippians 4:13, "I can do all things through Christ who strengthens me," then expand to Philippians 4:10-20 over time. Layering allows the truths to build upon one another.

Daily Repetition – Repetition is the key to retention. Write a verse on a notecard, place it on your mirror, and recite it every morning. Let it be the first thought that shapes your day.

IF MEMORIZATION PLANTS THE SEED, MEDITATION WATERS IT.

Visual Association – Use imagery to connect Scripture to your daily life. For instance, when memorizing Psalm 23:2, "He makes me lie down in green pastures," visualize yourself resting in a serene meadow with the Shepherd by your side.

Technological Tools – Apps like YouVersion or Bible Memory can aid your journey. Record yourself reading a verse and listen to it during commutes or while exercising. Let technology work for you.

If memorization plants the seed, meditation waters it. The Hebrew word for meditate is hagah, which means to murmur, muse, or ponder deeply. It's not passive reflection but an active engagement with the Word.

> This Book of the Law shall not depart from your mouth, but you shall meditate in it day and night, that you may observe to do according to all that is written in it. For then you will make your way prosperous, and then you will have good success. (Joshua 1:8)

Notice the connection: meditation leads to observation, which leads to transformation.

How to Meditate

1. Pause and Ponder – Take a single verse and read it slowly. Ask the Holy Spirit to highlight specific words or phrases. For example, with Psalm 46:10, "Be still, and know that I am God," focus on the command to "be still" and what that means in the current season of your life.

2. Speak It Out – Biblical meditation often involves verbal repetition. Speak the verse aloud, letting the Word saturate your environment. Declare it over your circumstances.

3. Journal Your Insights – As you meditate, write down the revelations that come. Journaling transforms fleeting thoughts into tangible reminders of God's voice.

4. Let meditation become immersive – Pray, sing, or even illustrate a verse. Turn it into an experience that resonates deeply within you.

Biblical meditation is rooted in the principle of abiding in Christ. The word "abide" in Greek is meno, which means to remain, dwell, or continue. When Jesus said, "Abide in Me, and I in you" (John 15:4), He was inviting us into continuous, intimate fellowship. When we meditate on Scripture, we're not merely performing a religious duty—we're entering into divine communion. The Holy Spirit takes the Word we're meditating on and makes it alive within us, transforming our thought

> **MEDITATION LEADS TO OBSERVATION, WHICH LEADS TO TRANSFORMATION.**

patterns and renewing our minds. This isn't just a mental exercise; it's a spiritual discipline that positions us to receive revelation and experience God's presence.

As we consistently meditate on His Word, allowing it to dwell richly within us, our thoughts align more closely with Heaven's perspective, and meditation becomes a cherished opportunity for intimate fellowship with our Father. Consider Isaac in Genesis 24:63, who went out into the field to meditate. During this quiet reflection, he encountered his future wife, Rebekah—a divine appointment that forever altered his life. Similarly, as we meditate, we position ourselves to receive Heaven's direction and provision.

Common Challenges and Solutions

Challenge: Lack of Time – Solution: Start small. Even five minutes of focused meditation can bring transformation. Redeem idle moments, like waiting in line, to rehearse Scripture.

Challenge: Distractions – Solution: Create a sacred space. Dedicate a quiet corner of your home as your meditation spot. Use instrumental worship music to set the atmosphere.

Challenge: Feeling Discouraged – Solution: Celebrate small victories. Every verse memorized and every moment meditating brings you closer to God's heart. Progress, not perfection, is the goal.

Memorization and meditation are not ends in themselves but pathways to transformation. As we internalize the Word, our thoughts, emotions, and decisions are conformed to God's will. We begin to think with Heaven's perspective and respond to life's challenges with supernatural peace and authority.

The Psalmist beautifully captures the reward:

> But his delight is in the law of the Lord, and in His law he meditates day and night. He shall be like a tree planted by the rivers of water, that brings forth its fruit in its season, whose leaf also shall not wither; and whatever he does shall prosper. (Psalm 1:2-3)

When we delight in God's Word, we become rooted in His presence, flourishing in every season of life.

As we develop these disciplines, they prepare us for the next step in our spiritual growth: deepening our prayer life. In the next chapter, we will explore how prayer transforms our relationship with God and equips us to bring Heaven's realities to Earth.

PROGRESS, NOT PERFECTION, IS THE GOAL.

Prayer for Meditation

Father, give us the discipline to meditate in Your Word "day and night." As I memorize Scripture, let it renew my mind and transform my life. Holy Spirit, breathe on every verse I study, bringing revelation and wisdom. Teach me to hide Your Word in my heart that it bears fruit pleasing to You. May Your Word guide me, anchor me, and draw me deeper into Your presence. I receive it by faith, in Jesus' name. Amen.

CHAPTER TEN

LORD, TEACH US TO PRAY

Prayer remains one of the most vital yet often misunderstood aspects of our relationship with God. Just as Jesus' disciples asked Him to teach them to pray, we must learn to communicate meaningfully with our Heavenly Father. This chapter explores the model prayer Jesus provided, offering practical insights into developing a vibrant prayer life that connects us with God's heart and purposes.

The model prayer resulted from a question by one of Jesus' disciples. One disciple saw that Jesus prayed in a way he had not known and asked, "Lord, teach us to pray, as John also taught his disciples." In the context of Scripture, Jesus then said to them:

> When you pray, say: Our Father in Heaven, Hallowed be Your name. Your Kingdom comes. Your will be done On earth as it is in Heaven. Give us day by day our daily bread. And forgive us

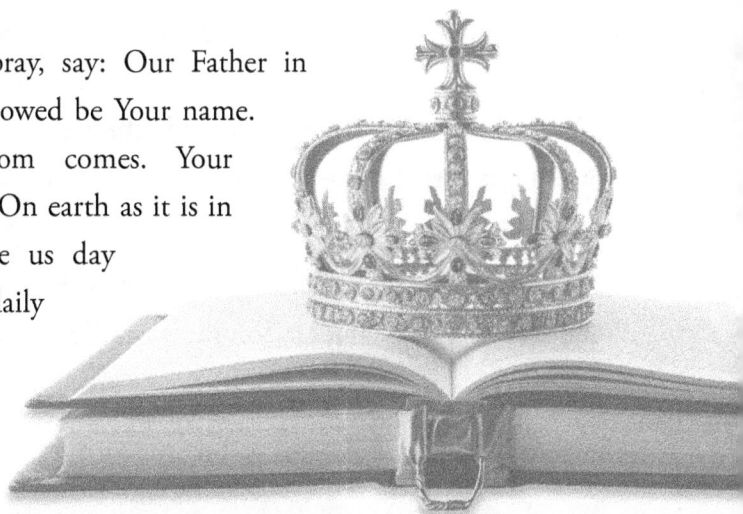

our sins, For we also forgive everyone who is indebted to us. And do not lead us into temptation, But deliver us from the evil one. (Luke 11:2-4 NKJV)

The Scriptures teach us to go line by line, precept by precept. Let's look at these verses a bit closer. In the Kingdom of God, God is our Father. Jesus begins this prophetic pattern of prayer by instructing the disciples to call on their Father. When Jesus called on "our Father," He acknowledged not only that He was the Son of God but also that the disciples were children of God and that they should come to the Father in this manner. When we pray "our Father," we are declaring that we, too, are sons of God and spiritual brothers and sisters in the Kingdom of God. When we pray "our Father," we are declaring we are a part of the family of God. This familial language used in the Lord's prayer also reminds us of the intimate relationship we have with God. We are not just servants or subjects but beloved children who can approach our Father with boldness and confidence.

By calling on "our Father," we are acknowledging that God is not just a distant deity but a loving parent who desires to be intimately involved in every aspect of our lives. This understanding changes how we view prayer; it becomes a conversation with our Heavenly Father rather than a one-sided monologue. As children of God, we also inherit certain privileges and responsibilities. Just as earthly children represent their parents and their family name, we, too, carry the name of Christ as ambassadors of His Kingdom. Our prayers should reflect this representation, seeking not just our desires but also faithfully upholding the will and purposes of God's Kingdom.

Also, we understand that all people are God's children because of creation, but not all are God's children according to redemption. The original family of God was broken by Adam and Eve, and due to rebellion against the Word of God, humanity became members of an alien family with Satan as their father (Gen. 3).

I'm reminded of a discourse where Jesus spoke with the Pharisees concerning them claiming to be the descendants of Abraham. Jesus declared to them that their issue was that they didn't receive His Word. Jesus said to them, "I speak what I have seen with My Father, and you do what you have seen with your father." The Pharisees told Jesus that Abraham was their father, but Jesus responded by letting them know if Abraham was their father, they'd do what he (Abraham) did and not attempt to kill Jesus.

Jesus then says the following:

> You do the deeds of your father. Then they said to Him, "We were not born of fornication; we have one Father— God." Jesus said to them, "If God were your Father, you would love Me, for I proceeded forth and came from God; nor have I come of Myself, but He sent Me. Why do you not understand My speech? Because you are not able to listen to My word. You are of your father the devil, and the desires of your father you want to do. He was a murderer from the beginning, and does not stand in the truth, because there is no truth in him. When he speaks a lie, he speaks from his own resources, for he is a liar and the father of it. (John 8:41-44 NKJV)

It's vitally important that we know we are children of the Highest God, our Heavenly Father. Jesus makes it clear that our actions and attitudes reveal who our true Father is. If we claim to be children of God yet do not love Jesus or follow His teachings, then we are not truly of God. Our love for Jesus and obedience to Him, even in prayer, is evidence of our relationship with God, the Father.

Abba Father

According to Scripture, up until this point, God was acknowledged as the Holy One of Israel, the Supreme Being far removed in the heavens—inaccessible and unapproachable. But I want you to be encouraged. You and I know Him as a loving, Heavenly Father who desires to live in intimate fellowship and communion with His children.

Throughout the ages, Abraham, Moses, Joshua, Elijah, David, and other Old Testament prophets and saints directed their prayers to the One true and living God, the all-powerful Jehovah. They knew Him as the Almighty God who revealed Himself with signs and wonders, rolled back the Red Sea, led them through the wilderness, rained down manna from Heaven, caused the waters to come from the rock, rained down fire from Heaven, delivered the three Hebrew boys from the fiery furnace, shut the mouths of lions and fought for and delivered them out of the hands of their enemies. But the Old Testament believers never prayed to God as their Father. They never cried out, "Abba Father!" as the New Testament believers do.

This shift in our relationship with God was made possible through Jesus Christ, who came to Earth as a man and sacrificed Himself for our sins. Through His death and resurrection, He bridged the gap between humanity and God, enabling us to have a personal relationship with our Heavenly Father.

Hallowed Be Your Name

The model prayer declared, "Hallowed be Your name." Hallowed has to do with adoration, honor, and the sanctifying of His name. In the Kingdom of God, our Father is our everything, and when we come to Him in prayer, we express that there is no one greater. Today, there are many great gospel songs, but there is a song I'm reminded by the artist Vashawn Mitchell, "Nobody Greater." What's even more impactful is that the Greater One lives within you.

When we pray, we establish the Kingdom of God on Earth. It was previously mentioned the word Kingdom means the way God does things, His rule, reign, royalty, and dominion. "Hallowed be Your name," according to Hebrew study, also means "to sanctify the name" or "to give one's life for his faith." This means we live out God's hallowedness not only in prayer, praise, and worship but by living a life pleasing to God. In the Scriptures, we are taught to be living sacrifices, holy and acceptable unto Him, which is our reasonable service or worship (Rom. 12:1). We know that the only way to accomplish this is by faith in the finished work of Jesus Christ.

WHEN WE PRAY, WE ESTABLISH THE KINGDOM OF GOD ON EARTH.

But know that the concept of "Hallowed be Your name" goes beyond just reciting words in prayer. It is a declaration of the holiness and greatness of God, acknowledging that He alone is worthy of our adoration and honor. As believers, we are called to not only express this in our prayer life but also through how we live our lives in the Kingdom.

The Bible teaches us that we are to be set apart for God's purposes and live according to His ways. This includes sanctifying or setting apart His name by how we conduct ourselves and represent Him to the world. Our actions should reflect the holiness of God and bring Him glory. I submit to you that we should always be reminded that as followers of Christ, we are called to live sacrificially and be willing to lay down our lives for the sake of the Gospel. This is the Kingdom way.

Your Kingdom Come

The model prayer declared, "Your Kingdom come." Our prayers should be focused on the Kingdom of God, not solely on our individual, organizational, or even denominational needs and desires. We call on God to fulfill His plan for our lives on Earth. "Your Kingdom come" is more than a desire for Christ to return and establish His Kingdom on Earth but that the anointing of Christ will reign in the lives of every believer and non-believer and in the entire earth. Earlier in this book, we stated that Jesus taught that the Kingdom of God was to be within us. The Greek verb tense used here is one of declaration meaning, "Come, Thy Kingdom." What am I saying?

This declaration of the model prayer is a reminder to prioritize God's Kingdom above all else. It is a call for His will to be done on Earth as it is in Heaven. This is why the words that we speak are so important in this very hour. The Scripture says:

> Forever, O Lord, Your word is settled in Heaven.
> (Psalm 119:89 NKJV)

I want you to notice that God's Word is settled in Heaven, not in the earth. It's not settled on the earth until someone on Earth says what God is saying from Heaven. In another place, Jesus said:

Assuredly, I say to you, whatever you bind on earth will be bound in Heaven, and whatever you loose on earth will be loosed in heaven. (Matthew 18:18 NKJV)

As Kingdom citizens, we have been given delegated authority by Christ Jesus to decree God's Word even in prayer and expect Heaven to back us up. As believers, we are called to live out this Kingdom mindset in our daily lives. But what exactly does "Your Kingdom come" mean? It means living according to God's principles and values, seeking first His righteousness, and bringing His light into the world. It involves loving others, serving those in need, and reflecting Christ's love and grace. These truths materialize in the lives of every believer when we pray. This leads us right into the next portion of Scripture.

Your Will Be Done

The model prayer declared, "Your will be done on earth as it is in Heaven." This decree is not a prayer to be made with thoughts that something unpleasant is going to happen in your lives, with fearful reservations or with anxiety, frustration, and tension. It's a shout of victory for God's children. We can speak the Word by faith over every area of our lives and be assured that He will guide us in each decision we make.

This declaration is saying to our Father that He reigns over every circumstance and situation because God's Kingdom is governed sovereignly and absolutely by His Word. We're decreeing that God's will be done on Earth as it is in Heaven. We're saying that God's plan for our lives on Earth is a pattern of His divine order in Heaven. Remember, Heaven provides the pattern for Earth in that His will is to be done with thanksgiving and obedience; this should be our objective. As we understand that God's

Kingdom resides within us, we know that what goes on internally lays the foundation for what occurs externally. It materializes by faith.

Our prayer for God's will to be done should not just be a theoretical concept. It should have practical implications in our daily lives. This means that we need to align our thoughts, words, and actions with the will and Word of God. This is why we must be walking in our purpose. As you are walking with God and hearing His voice, even in times of uncertainty, you'll know that you're where you're supposed to be and doing what you're supposed to be doing. The Scripture teaches us that the Holy Spirit works with the Word of God, and the Word of God works with the Spirit of God. As we keep Him first, the Kingdom of God will be a reality.

When we pray for His will to be done, we are surrendering our desires and plans to Him. We acknowledge that He knows what is best for us and trust that He will guide us in the right direction. For God's will to be done on Earth as it is in Heaven, we must also actively seek His wisdom. This involves spending time in prayer and reading the Word of God regularly. Apostle James teaches that if any man lacks wisdom, he is to ask of God, who gives wisdom to all liberally and will not withhold it (James 1). As we deepen our relationship with Him, His will becomes clearer to us.

THIS IS WHY WE MUST BE WALKING IN OUR PURPOSE.

When we make decisions or face challenges, it is important to seek God's will and not just rely on our understanding, even our own experiences. As new creations in Christ Jesus, we know that all things are of God now that we've been born again, and He makes all things new, even our ability to trust Him. Proverbs 3:5-6 reminds us to trust in the Lord with all our heart and lean not on our understanding, but in all our ways acknowledge Him, and He will direct our paths.

Ultimately, praying for God's will to be done on Earth as it is in Heaven reflects a heart of submission and obedience to God. It shows that we truly desire His Kingdom to come and His will to be done in every aspect of our lives. We are vessels for God's will, and it is a privilege and responsibility to carry out His plans on Earth. As we align ourselves with His will, we become instruments of change and can impact the world around us for His glory.

Our Daily Bread

The model prayer goes on to say, "Give us this day our daily bread." Jesus said to request that the Father release our daily bread or daily provision to us. Daily provision can come in a plethora of ways. This could be food on our tables, clothing, transportation, healing of our bodies, or breakthroughs in finance. Whatever it is that is needed in life for your daily needs, Jesus says when we acknowledge the Father and ask for His divine assistance, it will be given. It's given by the Father because He is our source. It's said so much in church simply because it is true that God, the Father, is our source; yet our paychecks, bank accounts, IRAs, stocks, bonds, or even family inheritances are the resources. The Word of God says:

> Yet for us there is but one God, the Father, who is the source of all things, and we *exist* for Him; and one Lord, Jesus Christ, by whom are all things [that have been created], and we [believers exist and have life and have been redeemed] through Him. (1 Corinthians 8:6 AMP)

The mere act of requesting our daily bread and provision from the Father uproots thoughts of selfishness or the idea that we can simply do things ourselves. It reveals a dependence on God in the hearts of the believer. The

Word "daily" in Greek means "necessary or essential bread, sufficient for our sustenance and support." Daily indicates that this should be prayed every day. I believe that Jesus was saying this because our Father is the great provider.

The word "bread" here has multiple meanings. Ezekiel 3:3 says, "Son of man," He said to me, "eat and fill your stomach with this scroll I am giving you." So, I ate, and it was as sweet as honey in my mouth." Jesus is described as the "bread of life" in John 6:35. This daily bread is a spiritual parallel of the Old Testament manna because, like manna, it is something collected daily and of which God is the source. Manna in Scripture was the substance miraculously supplied as food for the children of Israel in the wilderness. Manna means "What is it?" While manna met the physical needs of Israel, Moses emphasized that provision for spiritual needs was also necessary (Deut. 8:3). This dual nature does not diminish the daily bread of its spiritual application but adds to it the practical dimension of earthly realities. Jesus said it this way:

> It is written, 'Man shall not live by bread alone, but by every word that proceeds from the mouth of God.'
> (Matthew 4:4 NKJV)

The concept of daily bread also highlights the importance of living in the present moment and trusting in God for our needs. It reminds us not to worry about tomorrow but instead focus on today and trust that God will provide for us each day. In addition, praying for daily bread can serve as a reminder to be thankful for what we have been given. It is an act of acknowledging that everything we have comes from God and that it is not by our strength or efforts that we have provision.

Forgive Us Our Sins

The model prayer also says, "And forgive us our sins, for we also forgive everyone who is indebted to us." The word "forgiveness" in Greek is the word *aphesis,* which means something sent away; remission, releasing someone from obligation or debt. We need to take a serious look into the need to forgive. In prayer, it is important to posture our hearts in a place of forgiveness. Harboring hate, bitterness, or strife will always interfere with our honest and sincere worship before God. So, Jesus' instruction was to receive forgiveness and give forgiveness to others.

If we are to engage in this portion of the prayer, we must examine the significance of "forgiveness." To advance in the Kingdom of God, it is vitally important to release ALL hurt, pain, disappointment, and discouragement—among other aspects of darkness—from the heart.

I want you to take a moment right here and release anyone from your heart who has hindered your walk with God. Over the years, I've had to do the same. Some situations are more in-depth than others and require more time and prayer to fully let go of, but I know that God wants us to have a heart free from bitterness and resentment toward others.

Releasing past hurts and forgiving those who have wronged us is not easy. It requires courage, vulnerability, and a willingness to let go of our pride and hurt feelings. However, it is necessary for our spiritual growth and well-being. When we hold onto grudges and refuse to forgive, we allow others' actions to continue controlling our thoughts and emotions. We become prisoners of our pain.

Let's look at it from Jesus' perspective. Jesus had multiple opportunities to be offended. His family doubted who He was, religious leaders said He was teaching heresies, He was not accepted in His hometown as a

Prophet, and the multitudes who followed Him were more concerned with physical food than spiritual truths. Peter denied Him, Judas betrayed Him, and He suffered the humiliation and pain of death by crucifixion (modern-day capital punishment). We must learn to both receive and give forgiveness for personal offenses and injustices.

Forgiveness is a crucial aspect of our spiritual journey and relationship with God. It not only frees us from the burden of holding onto negative emotions and feelings, but it also aligns us with His heart and His will for our lives. Forgiveness is so important that Jesus spoke about it multiple times in His teachings. Matthew 6:14-15 informs us, "For if you forgive other people when they sin against you, your heavenly Father will also forgive you. But if you do not forgive others their sins, your Father will not forgive your sins." This shows the seriousness of harboring unforgiveness in our hearts.

FORGIVENESS DOESN'T MEAN WE HAVE TO FORGET OR EXCUSE THE WRONGDOING.

Forgiveness is not just an act we do for others but also an act of obedience to God. Colossians 3:13 says, "Bear with each other and forgive one another if any of you has a grievance against someone. Forgive as the Lord forgave you." We are called to forgive just as God has forgiven us by sending His Son to be our substitutionary sacrifice.

Forgiveness doesn't mean we have to forget or excuse the wrongdoing. It simply means releasing the negative emotions attached to the situation and entrusting justice to God. As human beings, it may be difficult for us to fully understand and accept this concept, but that's where faith and trust in God come in.

> Repay no one evil for evil. Have regard for good things in the sight of all men. If it is possible, as much as depends on

you, live peaceably with all men. Beloved, do not avenge yourselves, but rather give place to wrath; for it is written, "Vengeance is Mine, I will repay," says the Lord.

(Romans 12:17-19 NKJV)

Forgiveness also allows for healing and restoration in relationships. When we choose to forgive, we open the possibility for reconciliation and rebuilding trust with others. This doesn't mean that everything will go back to the way it was before, but it does pave the way for a healthier and more positive relationship moving forward.

Forgiveness is a continuous process rather than a one-time event. It may take time and effort to truly let go of hurt and bitterness, but as believers, we have the Holy Spirit within us to guide and help us in this journey towards forgiveness. So, make the conscious decision to forgive others as God has forgiven us. Remember that forgiveness is not just about those who have wronged us, but it benefits us and allows us to live in the freedom and peace that God desires for us. Now, I want you to also extend this same forgiveness towards yourselves, remembering that we are all imperfect and in need of God's grace.

Continuing the topic of forgiveness, it is important to address the misconception that forgiving someone means condoning their actions or letting them off the hook for their wrongdoings. This is not true. Forgiveness does not negate accountability or justice for what has been done. Forgiveness can bring about a sense of justice as we trust in God's perfect judgment and ultimate justice. We can take comfort in knowing that everyone will be held accountable for their actions before God.

EVERYONE WILL BE HELD ACCOUNTABLE FOR THEIR ACTIONS BEFORE GOD.

It is important to remember that forgiveness does not always mean reconciliation. In some cases, it may be necessary to maintain healthy boundaries and distance from those who have hurt us. However, we can still choose to forgive them in our hearts and release any anger or bitterness towards them.

The act of forgiveness requires humility, grace, and a willingness to let go of our desires for retribution. As we learn to forgive others as God has forgiven us, we also grow in our relationship with Him and reflect His love and mercy towards others. We should open our hearts to extending forgiveness as we continue this journey of faith. Make the conscious decision to forgive others and ourselves, recognizing the incredible gift of forgiveness that we have received through Jesus Christ.

It doesn't hurt to seek reconciliation where possible, showing the world the transformative power of forgiveness in our lives. Continuing to walk in forgiveness heals our hearts and relationships and ultimately leads us closer to God's perfect love and grace. Therefore, we should extend forgiveness not just as a one-time act but as an ongoing practice in our daily lives, reflecting the heart of our loving Father, who has forgiven us completely. Choose to forgive and experience true freedom in Christ.

Do Not Lead Us into Temptation

The model prayer also says, "Do not lead us into temptation." James the Apostle indicates that God does not tempt man; our Heavenly Father is not the tempter.

> Let no one say when he is tempted, 'I am tempted by God;' for God cannot be tempted by evil, nor does He tempt anyone. (James 1:13)

The Bible reveals that Satan is the tempter (Matt. 4:3, 1 Thess. 3:5) and explains this:

> Each one is tempted when he is drawn away by his own desires and enticed. Then, when desire has conceived, it gives birth to sin; and sin, when it is full-grown, brings forth death. (James 1:14-15)

Satan is the tempter, but we are drawn into his snare when we allow our fleshly desires to entice us. According to Scripture, those desires birth sin, and sin results in death. Some of Satan's attacks arise from uncontrolled evil desires from within. Jesus taught in Matthew 15 that it's not what's without that defiles a man, but what's in the heart. But I submit to you that other temptations come from without through our senses—hearing, seeing, feeling, touching, and tasting. Apostle Paul says:

WE ARE DRAWN INTO HIS SNARE WHEN WE ALLOW OUR FLESHLY DESIRES TO ENTICE US.

> No temptation has overtaken you except such as is common to man, but God is faithful, who will not allow you to be tempted beyond what you are able, but with the temptation will also make the way of escape, that you may be able to bear it. (1 Corinthians 10:13 NKJV)

We need to understand that the word temptation means "common." But be assured that it is possible to successfully overcome temptation or what is deemed common; to those who do so, God makes this decree toward us:

> Blessed is the man who endures temptation; for when he has been approved, he will receive the crown of life which the Lord has promised to those who love Him.
>
> (James 1:12)

With this revelation, I challenge you to begin declaring that you will receive the crown of life because you love the Lord more than anything. What a glorious insight to realize that you love God more than this whole world.

Jesus encouraged the disciples in prayer to ask the Father to keep them from tempting situations and deliver them from the "evil one." Here we see that it is the job of the adversary to distract, mislead, and attempt to stifle the child of God. So, we are to pray for deliverance from the plots, traps, and schemes of the enemy.

In the book of Ephesians, the apostle Paul says that we are to put on the whole armor of God to stand against the "wiles" of the enemy. Paul emphasizes that battles are not natural and that natural weapons are ineffective. Spiritual battles must be fought with spiritual weapons. Recently, the Spirit of the Lord came to me and reminded me that we should put on the full armor daily. We must clothe ourselves with our spiritual armor and protect ourselves with the anointing of Christ Jesus.

SPIRITUAL BATTLES MUST BE FOUGHT WITH SPIRITUAL WEAPONS.

To fully understand and apply this teaching, we must first recognize that there is a spiritual realm where these battles take place. The enemy is not physical but rather spiritual and seeks to deceive and destroy us. Therefore, we cannot fight him with physical weapons. Instead, we are called to put on the full armor of God, which includes the belt of truth, the breastplate of righteousness, shoes of peace, the shield of faith, the helmet of salvation, and the sword of the Spirit, which is the Word of God (Ephesians 6:14-17). Each piece has its significance in protecting us from the attacks of the enemy.

The Kingdom. The Power. The Glory

Lastly, in the model prayer, Jesus instructs the disciples to remind the Father that it's His Kingdom in which they serve and it's His power and His glory "forever" in which they express their authority as Kingdom citizens. The understanding for us here is that we can claim the provisions, promises, and protection of this prayer because we, too, are His children. The glory of God gives us access to all that He is and all that He has. As a result, we have a covenant right by Christ Jesus as we acknowledge and agree with everything God says in His holy Word about His Kingdom. Remember what Jesus said:

> Behold, I give you the authority to trample on serpents and scorpions, and over all the power of the enemy, and nothing shall by any means hurt you. (Luke 10:19 NKJV)

This is a powerful reminder that we are not to be afraid or intimidated by his tactics because we have been given the ability to overcome them. We are representatives of His Kingdom here on earth. We carry the authority and power of His name wherever we go and whatever situation we may face.

Prayer aligns us with God's purposes and prepares us for faithful stewardship. In our final chapter, we'll learn how to manage everything God entrusts to us for Kingdom advancement.

The Model Prayer

Our Father in Heaven, hallowed be Your name. Your Kingdom come. Your will be done on Earth as it is in Heaven. Give us day by day our daily bread. And forgive us our sins, for we also forgive everyone who is indebted to us. And do not lead us into temptation, but deliver us from the evil one. I thank You for it. In Jesus' name. Amen.

CHAPTER ELEVEN

KINGDOM STEWARDSHIP

S tewardship extends far beyond managing money—it encompasses every resource God entrusts to us as citizens of His Kingdom. This chapter examines what it means to be faithful managers of God's provisions, whether material possessions, spiritual gifts, relationships, or opportunities. We'll discover how proper stewardship positions us to fulfill our purpose while advancing God's Kingdom on Earth.

Everything we own belongs to God as Kingdom citizens. We, being created in God's image and likeness, are stewards who manage God's wealth on Earth. The moment we accepted Christ, we became accountable for wisely using what God had committed to our trust.

This world has a way of portraying financial success and material possessions. But those views are promoted through social media, television, radio, and many other ways, which may distort the truth. However, God's way of viewing money involves a simple concept called

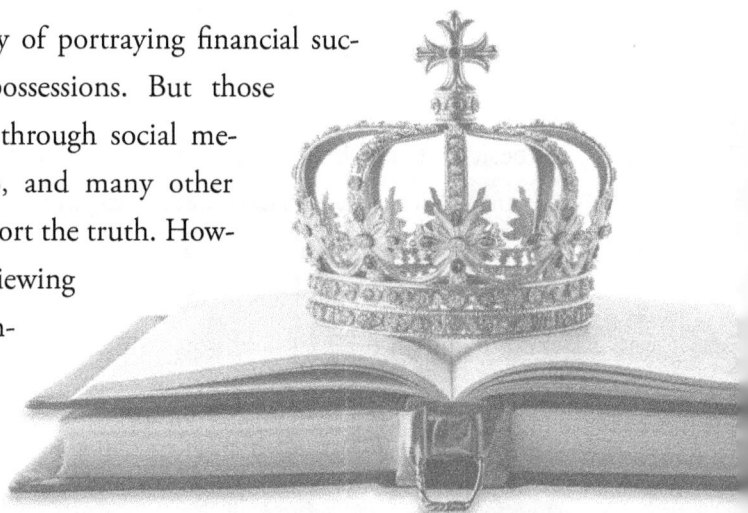

Kingdom stewardship, and this perspective is made available to us according to the Scriptures.

Parable of the Talents

> For the Kingdom of Heaven is like a man traveling to a far country, who called his own servants and delivered his goods to them. And to one he gave five talents, to another two, and to another one, to each according to his own ability; and immediately he went on a journey. Then he who had received the five talents went and traded with them and made another five talents. And likewise he who had received two gained two more also. But he who had received one went and dug in the ground and hid his lord's money. After a long time the lord of those servants came and settled accounts with them. So he who had received five talents came and brought five other talents, saying, 'Lord, you delivered to me five talents; look, I have gained five more talents besides them.' His lord said to him, 'Well done, good and faithful servant; you were faithful over a few things, I will make you ruler over many things. Enter into the joy of your lord.' He also who had received two talents came and said, 'Lord, you delivered to me two talents; look, I have gained two more talents besides them.' His lord said to him, 'Well done, good and faithful servant; you have been faithful over a few things, I will make you ruler over many things. Enter the joy of your lord.' Then he who had received the one talent came and said, 'Lord, I knew you to be a hard man, reaping

where you have not sown, and gathering where you have not scattered seed. And I was afraid and went and hid your talent in the ground. Look, there you have what is yours.' But his lord answered and said to him, 'You wicked and lazy servant, you knew that I reap where I have not sown and gather where I have not scattered seed. So you ought to have deposited my money with the bankers, and at my coming I would have received back my own with interest. So take the talent from him and give it to him who has ten talents. For to everyone who has, more will be given, and he will have abundance; but from him who does not have, even what he has will be taken away. And cast the unprofitable servant into the outer darkness. There will be weeping and gnashing of teeth. Jesus begins this discourse by stating that this text is likened to the Kingdom of Heaven. In other Words, If you and I have ears to hear what the Spirit of the Lord is saying then we recognize in Jesus' teaching that we have an opportunity to materialize Heaven on earth as Kingdom citizens.

(Matthew 25:14-30)

Jesus teaches that this man who is to travel to a far country calls his servants and delivers his goods to them before his departure. We believe here that "the man" is a representation of Christ Himself, who is to return to Heaven but be crucified, resurrected, and seated on the right hand of the Father before returning to Earth in His second coming. By revelation, Apostle Paul says the following to the church of Ephesus regarding the grace gifts Christ gave to men:

> And He Himself gave some *to be* apostles, some prophets,
> some evangelists, and some pastors and teachers.
>
> (Ephesians 4:11 NKJV)

I submit to you that Christ illustrates this in the book of Matthew because the Jewish leaders of that time rejected Him as a Messiah. However, He desired that they acknowledge that He came to give grace gifts to humankind as Lord and Savior, even eternal life.

In the illustration, the man called his servants to commit goods to their trust and their management. I want you to notice the Scripture said, "his goods." He delivered "his goods" to them. In this case, the servants were expected to use their master's money or gifts in trade and to make as large of an increase with what they'd been given as possible. The term "goods" here represents several understandings.

First, "goods" represent the gospel, the divine truths, or the gifts to decree these truths to men. Secondly, "goods" represent the gifts or endowments conferred for a spiritual end, powers of body and mind, abilities natural and acquired, health, understanding, wealth, and every advantage of which good or bad use may be made. We see this clarified in the text as two servants doubled their talents, and the servant with one talent buried his talent in the earth.

Thirdly, "goods" represent what God has given us and our ability to be good stewards of God's wealth. God's wealth includes the ability, talent, or gift He's given us and our willingness to produce it on Earth. In the beginning, when God created man, He spoke into man and gave him the ability to be fruitful, which is another word for production. God called it fruitfulness.

Then God blessed them, and God said to them, "Be fruitful and multiply; fill the earth and subdue it; have dominion over the fish of the sea, over the birds of the air, and over every living thing that moves on the earth.

(Genesis 1:28 NKJV)

God desires us to be fruitful and increase. He desires us to multiply what He's given us again as good stewards. Going further into the text. The man gives the servants talents according to "their ability." He apportioned his gifts following his knowledge of the servants' capacity for business and Kingdom stewardship. We know that God distributes His endowments in such proportions as men can bear and profit from. The unlimited variety in men's dispositions, intellects, wills, opportunities, and positions are considered to include the level of their responsibility. In other words, God won't give you more than you can handle.

The man gives talents according to the servant's ability or natural capacity to increase and use their gift. What does this mean for you and me? Each of us has a unique set of talents and gifts that are specifically designed, by God, to help us fulfill our purpose in life. It is our responsibility to recognize and cultivate these gifts, so that we may use them for the glory of God and the advancement of His Kingdom.

This parable also teaches us about the importance of stewardship. Just as the servants were given a specific number of talents to steward, we are also entrusted with resources from God that we must manage wisely and responsibly. This includes not only our talents and abilities but also our time, finances, relationships, and other blessings in life.

IT IS OUR RESPONSIBILITY TO RECOGNIZE AND CULTIVATE THESE GIFTS

To be good stewards, we must first acknowledge that everything we have belongs to God. We are merely caretakers or managers of His possessions on Earth. As such, it is our duty to use these resources, talents, and gifts in a way that aligns with God's will and honors Him. This may even require wisdom, discernment, selflessness, and other attributes of the Holy Spirit.

The man left each servant to use the gifts and talents assigned to him uncontrolled and undirected. This means that God is looking at our faithfulness and trustworthiness. The servants who were given five talents and two talents, respectively, both traded and gained twice as much as their master had given them. They found business partners who were good stewards and engaged in growth opportunities. The message here is that there is great significance in using your gift as a seed to the Lord.

We see here that God rewards faithfulness. Another major lesson is that the servants had to account for what they did with what was given to them. The Scriptures teach us the importance and significance of stewardship, which includes accountability.

The servants who had five talents and two talents, respectively, received good reviews from their master upon his return:

> Well done, good and faithful servant; you have been faithful over a few things, I will make you ruler over many things. Enter into the joy of your lord.
>
> (Matthew 25:23 NKJV)

In other words, they were profitable. We see that faithfulness leads to success. They had multiplied their talents, and as a result, they were rewarded with even more responsibility and blessings. This is a great lesson for us to learn in our own lives; being faithful in the little things can lead to greater opportunities and blessings.

The servant who had one talent buried his talent in the ground, alleging that he knew his master was a hard man reaping where he had not sowed, alleging that this then made him afraid. The servant attempted to offer his talent back to his master. What we notice here in the text is what is called an unprofitable servant. This servant lied to himself, made an excuse, and chose to do nothing with what was given to him. He was not faithful and did not use his talents to bring profit to his master. This unprofitable servant represents those who choose to ignore their responsibilities and potential, making excuses for why they can't do more or succeed. They let fear hold them back from taking risks and using what they have been given. This leads to missed opportunities and a lack of growth in their lives.

As Kingdom citizens, we are called to be profitable servants, using our God-given talents and abilities for His glory. We should strive to be faithful to what we have been given, knowing that our faithfulness will earn us even greater blessings and responsibilities from God.

I encourage you to write that book, start a real estate career, purchase stocks and bonds, enter Kingdom entrepreneurship, start your business, and consider becoming a keynote speaker. Whatever you do, do it as unto the Lord. In your faithfulness, God will reward you.

Kingdom Economics

Throughout Scripture, we see that God's economic blueprint is marked by divine wisdom, integrity, and generational impact. Abraham's covenant included blessings of wealth, but that wealth came with a purpose: to bless all nations (Genesis 12:2-3). Solomon, in all his wisdom, demonstrated the integration of spiritual insight and practical application in his trade and governance. These biblical examples remind us that God is intensely interested in how His people manage resources.

We must understand that wealth, influence, and opportunity are tools for advancing Heaven's agenda on Earth. When we embrace this perspective, we shift from being owners to being stewards. This shift unlocks supernatural provision and positions us for greater influence.

IN YOUR FAITHFULNESS, GOD WILL REWARD YOU.

Stewarding finances according to Kingdom principles often requires unlearning the ways of the world. Proverbs 13:11 reminds us, "Wealth gained by dishonesty will be diminished, but he who gathers by labor will increase." This Scripture underscores the importance of integrity and diligence in financial matters.

Faithful stewardship positions us to manage resources and multiply them for eternal purposes. When we align with God's principles, we partner with Heaven to see supernatural results—results that affect not just our generation but those to come.

I submit to you that when we live with eternity in mind, our entire approach to stewardship transforms. This eternal perspective fundamentally changes how we view and manage every resource God entrusts to us.

> While we do not look at the things which are seen, but at the things which are not seen. For the things which are seen are temporary, but the things which are not seen are eternal. (2 Corinthians 4:18).

When we grasp this eternal reality, every business decision becomes an act of worship, and every financial investment is a seed sown into eternal soil. The word "steward" in Greek is oikonomos, which means a manager of household affairs. This emphasizes our role as caretakers rather than owners. This understanding transforms our approach to business endeavors, financial decisions, and Kingdom opportunities. We begin to see that everything we manage today has eternal implications—every choice either advances or hinders God's Kingdom purposes.

Just as Abraham looked for a city whose builder and maker was God (Hebrews 11:10), we must conduct our affairs with Heaven's perspective. We must know that our faithful stewardship today ripples into eternity. When we align our business and financial decisions with God's eternal purposes, we position ourselves for both prosperity on Earth and eternal rewards.

While faithful stewardship positions us for Kingdom advancement individually, God designed us to multiply our impact through authentic community. In Chapter 12, we'll discover how to build and nurture the life-giving relationships that amplify our Kingdom influence.

Prayer for Kingdom Stewardship

Father, You are the giver of life and source of all things. I know that all I have received is from Your hand. Gracious and loving God, You've called me to be a steward of Your abundance, a caretaker of all You have entrusted to me. Help me to always use my gifts wisely and teach me to share them generously. Grant me wisdom to conduct my affairs according to Your principles. Grant me the courage to make decisions that honor You. Help me to see every economic opportunity through the Kingdom perspective. May my stewardship multiply resources for Your glory and extend Your influence in the marketplace. Guide me in creating wealth with purpose and transferring inheritance with Kingdom values. I thank You for it now, and I receive it by faith, in Jesus' name. Amen.

CHAPTER TWELVE

THE POWER OF KINGDOM COMMUNITY

The Christian faith was never meant to be lived in isolation. From the very beginning, when God declared, "It is not good for man to be alone" (Genesis 2:18), to the vibrant early church that gathered daily in homes and temple courts, Scripture consistently emphasizes the vital importance of community. The word "community" in Greek is *koinonia*, which means fellowship, communion, or partnership. This speaks to something far deeper than casual association—it represents covenant relationship and shared purpose in advancing God's Kingdom.

Recent studies reveal a troubling trend: church attendance in America has declined significantly. As of 2020, only about 47% of Americans belong to a house of worship, down from 70% in 1999. This decline directly contradicts God's design for His people. I submit to you that Kingdom power flows most powerfully through unified believers gathered in local churches. The word "church" in Greek is *ekklesia*, which means "the called-out ones" or "an assembly."

When the disciples gathered in the upper room at Pentecost, they weren't simply a collection of individuals seeking personal encounters—they were a unified community experiencing the outpouring of the Holy Spirit. The Greek word for "unity" here is *homothymadon*, which means "with one mind" or "with one accord." This same pattern continues throughout the Book of Acts, where signs, wonders, and dramatic conversions occur in the context of believers living, praying, and ministering together within established local assemblies.

THESE DIGITAL OPTIONS CANNOT FULLY REPLACE IN-PERSON FELLOWSHIP.

In our modern world of individualism and digital connections, many believers miss the transformative power of authentic Kingdom community found in a local church. While we're grateful for technology that allows live streaming and virtual services—especially during times of necessity like the COVID-19 pandemic or for those who are physically unable to attend due to illness, disability, deployment, or distance—these digital options cannot fully replace in-person fellowship. The Kingdom of God operates through covenant relationships—bonds that go deeper than convenience or common interests.

The Scripture declares that "from whom the whole body, joined and knit together by what every joint supplies, according to the effective working by which every part does its share, causes growth of the body for the edifying of itself in love" (Ephesians 4:16). The word "supplies" here is the Greek word *epichoregeo*, which means to furnish abundantly or to fully provide. Every member has something vital to contribute to the body's growth.

The Foundation of Biblical Community

The early church provides our model for Kingdom community. Acts 2:42 tells us, "And they continued steadfastly in the apostles' doctrine and fellowship, in the breaking of bread, and in prayers." The word "stead-fastly" here is the Greek word *proskartereo*, which means to persevere or to be constantly diligent. This wasn't casual or convenience-based commitment—it was deliberate, intentional devotion to building genuine community through regular assembly and shared life.

Kingdom community, expressed through active church involvement, serves multiple divine purposes that extend far beyond mere social connection or religious obligation. At its core, it facilitates spiritual growth through the principle of iron sharpening iron. The word "sharpen" in Hebrew is *chadad*, which means to be keen or alert. When believers walk closely together in a local church setting, their interactions naturally produce spiritual refinement.

Finding Your Church Home

I submit to you that finding and connecting with the right local church is essential for your spiritual growth and Kingdom advancement. When seeking a church home, the Holy Spirit will guide you to look for:

- Sound biblical teaching that aligns with God's Word
- A welcoming atmosphere where you can build genuine relationships
- Opportunities for spiritual growth and service
- Leadership that demonstrates godly character and vision
- Active community involvement and outreach

Regular church attendance is vital for spiritual development and Kingdom impact. The Scripture teaches us in Hebrews 10:25, "not forsaking the assembling of ourselves together, as is the manner of some, but exhorting one another, and so much the more as you see the Day approaching." The word "assembling" here is *episynagoge*, which speaks of a deliberate gathering together.

Developing Your Spiritual Gifts

God has equipped every believer with specific gifts for Kingdom service. Romans 12:6-8 outlines the motivational gifts: prophecy, serving, teaching, exhortation, giving, leadership, and mercy. The word "gift" here is the Greek word *charisma*, which refers to a divine endowment. These gifts are honed and developed through active participation in the local church.

THESE GIFTS ARE HONED AND DEVELOPED THROUGH ACTIVE PARTICIPATION IN THE LOCAL CHURCH.

The Apostle Paul teaches us that "the manifestation of the Spirit is given to each one for the profit of all" (1 Corinthians 12:7). Every part of the body is significant—whether seemingly prominent or humble in function. The eye cannot say to the hand, "I have no need of you," nor can the head say to the feet, "I have no need of you" (1 Corinthians 12:21). Each member's contribution is vital for the body's healthy functioning. Through consistent church attendance, you receive:

- Regular spiritual nourishment through the preached Word
- Protection and covering through godly leadership
- Opportunities for corporate worship and prayer
- Relationships that provide support and accountability
- Platform for discovering and using your spiritual gifts
- Structure for spiritual discipline and growth
- Opportunity to develop and exercise your motivational gifts

The Power of United Prayer and Worship

The community of believers, gathered regularly in local churches, creates an atmosphere where Kingdom power can flow more freely. Jesus promised, "For where two or three are gathered together in My name, I am there in the midst of them" (Matthew 18:20). The word "gathered" here is the Greek word *synago*, which means to bring together or assemble. While online streaming can facilitate connection, it cannot replicate the powerful dynamic of physical gathering for prayer and worship.

When believers stand together in faith, their spiritual authority multiplies. The early church demonstrated this reality as they prayed together for boldness, saw prison doors opened, and experienced miraculous provision. In Acts 4:31, after the believers prayed together, "the place where they were assembled together was shaken." The word "shaken" is the Greek word *saleuo*, which means to agitate or rock like a storm at sea. This demonstrates the raw power released through united prayer and worship in the gathered church.

> **WHEN BELIEVERS STAND TOGETHER IN FAITH, THEIR SPIRITUAL AUTHORITY MULTIPLIES.**

Building authentic community often faces obstacles. Time constraints, trust issues, past hurts, and cultural barriers can all hinder genuine connection and regular church attendance. Surveys indicate that many Americans now view church attendance as optional rather than essential, with only 28% of young adults considering regular attendance important for spiritual growth.

However, the Greek word for "overcome" is *nikao*, which means to conquer or prevail. Through Christ's love, power, and wisdom, we can overcome these challenges and build lasting, meaningful relationships within the local church. While virtual services may temporarily bridge gaps during exceptional circumstances, whenever possible, we must prioritize physical presence in our local assembly. This is where true body ministry occurs—where we can lay hands on the sick, embrace the hurting, and minister face-to-face as the early church did.

The Multiplication Effect

Healthy Kingdom communities centered in local churches naturally re-produce. This follows the biblical principle of multiplication, which is seen throughout Scripture, from God's command to "be fruitful and multiply" to Jesus's parable of the multiplying seed. The Greek word for "multiply" is *plethyno*, which suggests not just numerical increase but exponential growth.

I submit to you that building an authentic Kingdom community through active church involvement isn't optional—it's essential for fulfilling our divine mandate. The enemy understands this, which is why he works so hard to isolate believers and create division within churches. The word "division" in Greek is *dichostasia*, meaning dissension or standing apart. We must actively resist this strategy by forgiving, walking in love, developing fruit of the spirit, and intentionally building and maintaining strong King-dom relationships through faithful church attendance and participation.

Your spiritual growth accelerates when you're properly connected to the body of Christ. The Church isn't just an organization—it's a living organ-ism, the Body of Christ. By building genuine community through consis-tent church involvement, we position ourselves for greater manifestations of God's presence and power while extending His influence on the earth.

I encourage you to pray and seek God's direction in finding your church home. Once He leads you, commit yourself fully to that community. Get involved beyond Sunday services—join a small group, serve in a minis-try, and build relationships with fellow believers. The Kingdom of God advances through unified believers who understand and embrace their corporate identity and purpose within the local church.

Prayer for Kingdom Community

Father God, thank You for the gift of community and relationships. Help me find and connect with a local church where I can grow in Your purposes. Give me wisdom to overcome obstacles, courage to be vulnerable, strength to forgive, and love to sustain relationships. May our church communities demonstrate Your power and draw others into Your Kingdom. Guide me to a place of belonging where I can serve You effectively and build lasting Kingdom relationships. In Jesus' name. Amen.

CONCLUSION

Congratulations! You have completed *Welcome to the Kingdom*. Your journey of Kingdom citizenship transforms every aspect of life, from how you view yourself to how you interact with the world around you. Throughout this book, we've explored foundational truths that establish us in God's Kingdom.

It's time to take the next step in your walk with God by following the Lord in believers' baptism and joining a local, Bible-believing church. You will discover a new level of support from a caring Pastor and experience peace and joy in becoming involved in a loving church family.

Remember, this book isn't meant to be just another source of information—it's an invitation to experience the living reality of God's Kingdom. The principles we've discussed aren't merely theological concepts; they're keys that unlock supernatural living. As you implement these truths, you'll find yourself walking in greater authority, experiencing deeper peace, and manifesting more of God's power in your daily life.

To continue growing in these Kingdom principles, consider using the *Welcome to the Kingdom Workbook* to help you fully integrate these truths into your daily life. Through intentional reflection and practical application, you'll develop a stronger foundation in Kingdom living.

You may have been given this book at church. I encourage you to plan to attend the next service and take the opportunity to speak to the Pastor or another member. I'm sure they will be happy to help you continue your Christian growth. But also, you may have received this book from the person who led you to the Lord. Please talk to that person if you are unsure of how to find a Bible-believing house of worship.

Your citizenship in God's Kingdom isn't just about securing your eternal destiny—though that's certainly included. It's about representing Heaven's culture on Earth today. You are an ambassador of Christ, carrying His presence, power, and authority wherever you go. Every situation you encounter is an opportunity to demonstrate Kingdom principles and expand God's influence in your sphere.

The Bible tells us, "Of the increase of His government and peace there shall be no end" (Isaiah 9:7). This increase begins with individual believers like you who understand their identity and purpose in the Kingdom. As you continue to grow in these truths, you'll naturally influence others, creating a ripple effect that extends far beyond your immediate circle.

These Kingdom principles come alive when practiced in community with fellow believers. Share what you've learned with others. Put these teachings into practice. Most importantly, maintain an attitude of expectancy—God has so much more for you to discover and experience in His Kingdom.

Lastly, you can also connect with us. Our ministry is accessible online at www.ncmhouseofmiracles.com. Continue to study God's Word, deepen your prayer life, and watch for opportunities to demonstrate Kingdom power. Stay hungry for more of God's presence and seek to be sensitive to the leading of the Holy Spirit.

Welcome to the adventure of Kingdom living. The best is yet to come.

ACKNOWLEDGMENTS

To all the pastors, ministers, and spiritual leaders who tirelessly serve their communities and spread the message of love, hope, and salvation. Your dedication to God's work is truly commendable. Remember that each day is a new opportunity to grow closer to God and fulfill His purpose for your life. Let this book be a reminder that with faith in God, all things are possible.

To my friends and family who have always believed in me, thank you for your unwavering support and encouragement. Your love and faith in my abilities have helped me overcome every obstacle along the way. To the New Covenant Ministry (NCM) of Lancaster, CA family, I am extremely grateful for you all. Thank you for always providing a safe and loving community where we can grow in our faith together.

To Lady Vicki L. Kemp for her book coaching and consulting, as well as for her guidance and support in creating this book. Her wisdom and expertise have been invaluable throughout this process, and I am forever grateful for her mentorship.

I thank Christian Living Books, Inc. for their expertise, support, and encouragement in spreading the message of faith through literature. Their editorial team's dedication to excellence helped refine and strengthen this manuscript.

ABOUT THE AUTHOR

P astor Charles E. Meux, Jr. is a visionary lead- er dedicated to empowering individuals to achieve success and prosperity. Born in Sacramento, California, Charles attributes his bold determination to succeed and uplift others to the strong community and spiritual influences of his upbringing.

Charles attended the University of Phoenix, where he developed a keen interest in business. He served in the California Department of Corrections, rising to the rank of Correctional Captain over a 27-year career. In 2016, he transitioned into full-time ministry and, in 2023, concluded his esteemed career in corrections to dedicate himself wholly to the ministry of the Lord Jesus Christ full-time.

A graduate of Ephraim Life Bible College and Seminary with a Bachelor of

Theology, Charles is a spiritual son of Bishop Clarence E. McClendon, under whose ministry he has served for the past decade. He is also ordained through the Academy of Healing as part of Bishop McClendon's ministries and crusade team.

Charles is the Founder and Pastor of New Covenant Ministry in Lancaster, California. His church offers various programs, including a Food Outreach initiative, a dynamic Marriage Ministry, and a transformative Women's Empowerment Clinic.

He is the husband of one wife. He is married to Desiree and is a proud father of eight children: Charnae, Kyndall, Aurion, Desirae, Tye, Tyson, Tristin, and Christen.

Connect with Pastor Meux

IG – ncmhouseofmiracles

Facebook – New Covenant Ministry of Lancaster/House of Miracles

Website – www.ncmhouseofmiracles.com

Business Email – ncmwelcometothekingdom@gmail.com

www.ingramcontent.com/pod-product-compliance
Lightning Source LLC
Chambersburg PA
CBHW060350090426
42734CB00011B/2097